against

the

state

crispin sartwell

against the state

an introduction to anarchist political theory

state university of new york press

Published by

STATE UNIVERSITY OF NEW YORK PRESS, ALBANY

© 2008   State University of New York

For information, contact
State University of New York Press,
Albany, NY
www.sunypress.edu

Production, book design, Laurie Searl
Marketing, Michael Campochiaro

Library of Congress Cataloging-in-Publication Data

Sartwell, Crispin, 1958–
    Against the state : an introduction to anarchist
political theory / Crispin Sartwell.
        p. cm.
    Includes bibliographical references and index.
    ISBN 978-0-7914-7447-1 (hardcover : alk. paper)
    ISBN 978-0-7914-7448-8 (pbk. : alk. paper)
1. Anarchism. I. Title.

HX833.S27 2008
320.5'7—dc22

                                        2007033815

10   9   8   7   6   5   4   3   2   1

For my children—

Emma Sartwell, Hayes Winik, Vince Winik,

Sam Sartwell, and Jane Winik Sartwell—

in the hope that they will someday

live in a freer world.

There cannot exist good laws where there are no good armies.

Machiavelli, *The Prince*

Force shites upon reason's back.

Benjamin Franklin, *Poor Richard's Almanac*

contents

acknowledgments

I thank Marion Winik, who read this book in various versions and offered many ideas for improvements and corrections. I add that Marion Winik is no anarchist. This book emerged from my job teaching section after section of political philosophy at Dickinson College. I am grateful to that institution and in particular the Political Science department for giving me a job, and a job that forced me to traverse the classics of Western political philosophy a dozen times, growing ever more hostile to the texts in the process. And thanks to the students in these classes who spurred me to develop better arguments and state them more clearly. I taught an early version of the book to a senior seminar on anarchism at Dickinson, and revised it substantially because of that experience. I also owe a debt of gratitude to two anonymous reviewers for SUNY Press and to Jane Bunker and Laurie Searl. Jane and Laurie have tolerated my somewhat eccentric style and neglect of some scholarly niceties through a series of books that has been, in all seriousness, a pleasure to write and a surprise to see published.

part I

preliminaries

introduction

I

I've considered myself an anarchist since I was twelve. I read Marx and Engels's *Communist Manifesto*, thought I understood it, and spent a couple of months declaring myself to be a Marxist and a communist. Then I read Emma Goldman's *Anarchism* and Alexander Berkman's *The ABC of Communist Anarchism* and realized something which should have been obvious even to one of tender years: Marx was a totalitarian, an enemy of freedom. Even if there was to be an ecstasy at the end of history when there were no social classes and no need for state power, in the meantime there were to be, putting it mildly, executions. And since already at this point my main intuition was that authority was a problem and freedom the only worthy goal of politics, I converted.

Now anarchism is often portrayed as a kind of mental illness—a symptom rather than an opinion. Perhaps this is true, and my antipathy toward all authority—parental, scholastic, legal—no doubt has origins that could lead it to be diagnosed as a personality disorder. But in general, everyone's political philosophy is the result of a personality disorder, and I prefer the disorder that resists authority to those that constitute it. And even if my anarchism is a pathology,

3

it does not follow that it is false. Dismiss it as adolescent, if you like, so long as you admit that it's true.

I had a brief run as a sort of junior quasi-violent revolutionary, and a somewhat longer run as an agitator and pamphleteer during the death throes of the peace movement. The decades have seen a slow transformation into a philosophy professor and a decided bourgeois; these days I am an anarchist with an SUV, and in no way pursuing the violent overthrow of anything. This may be hypocritical, or it may not be, depending on your sense of what anarchism demands, but in any case if I have any contribution to make to the anarchist cause, it is at this point of my life a more or less purely intellectual one.

II

By *anarchism* I refer to the view that all forms of human association ought to be, as far as is possible, voluntary. Usually the word is thought to mean (where it is not thought merely to mean social chaos) the doctrine that government should not exist. To the extent that government is a nonvoluntary association— that is, to the extent that it rests on coercion—the meaning I give of 'anarchism' entails that government should not exist. But the emphasis on voluntariness also gives anarchism a more positive flavor, and captures some of the reasons that many idealists have been and continue to be inspired by the idea, even as many other people—including, I should add, other sorts of idealists—are repulsed by it.

The first and sometimes the only response to anarchism is that it is utterly impractical. Perhaps it will even be admitted that anarchism is an inspiring idea and that resort to force to create order is regrettable. Nevertheless, the objection continues, force is necessary because, among other things, people tend to be self-interested and even perversely destructive. As Thomas Paine (a man who had some sympathy with anarchism) said, government is produced by our wickedness. "For were the impulses of conscience clear, uniform, and irresistibly obeyed, man would need no other lawgiver; but that not being the case, he finds it necessary to surrender up a part of his property to furnish means for the protection of the rest; and this he is induced to do by the same prudence which in every other case advises him out of two evils to choose the least."[1]

Paine has the virtue of honesty in comparison with some views that puff up the state with quasi-cosmic mumbo-jumbo into a god on earth. At least he frankly admits that the state rests on coercion, and that, all things being equal, coercion is evil. But for Paine, since having one's life and property in a state of constant vulnerability is even more discomfiting, we choose coercion over anarchy. And the reason we are constantly vulnerable is because people have lost their innocence; fallen from the garden, we wallow in sin, understood as a tendency to take everything that is not nailed down and kill anyone who tries to stop us.

It is often said that anarchists have an unrealistically positive, or perhaps simply naïve view of human nature. And this has indeed been the case with many anarchist theorists: William Godwin and Emma Goldman spring to mind. Let the people go, these thinkers allege, and they will create a paradise on earth; it is precisely the coercive state and the repressive forces it represents which stunt and deform our nature. Free, each person becomes an artist of her own life. But to begin with, we do not have a clear idea of how people would behave without a state, though we might appeal to the example of tribal cultures. Through most of the history of our species—perhaps 98% of it—people lived without a state, but we are at the point where the coercive state actually appears to most people to be an unquestionable necessary condition of human existence. People can't quite grasp the idea that one is trying to throw the whole thing into question. This attitude, if nothing else does, makes anarchism unrealistic: no one can even imagine, much less want it. That is a testimony to the extent to which the state has been able to render us dependent, and the extent to which it has educated, hectored, indoctrinated, beaten, nurtured, and executed us into taking it to be the only normal condition of human beings.

It is worth taking seriously some of the reasons anarchists have believed that people would be better without a state. Emerson, for example, thought the state a great barrier to self-reliance and self-discipline: "Wild liberty develops iron conscience. Want of liberty, by strengthening law and decorum, stupefies conscience"[2] One gets in the habit of deferring to authority, which promises to relieve one of responsibility for one's decisions, starting with the decision of obedience. There is no use for self-discipline in a situation in which there is overwhelming external coercion, and people can want to be coerced precisely to relieve themselves of the necessity of controlling themselves. Of course that in itself shows human nature as something at a minimum weak, if not intrinsically corrupt.

Here, I do not intend to assume that people are basically benevolent. I do think that people are capable of benevolence, of doing good things for other people for basically unselfish reasons, but I acknowledge that, wherever you have people, rape, robbery, and murder follow. It is not at all true that all versions of anarchism depend on a positive view of human nature; many anarchist thinkers, including Pierre-Joseph Proudhon—probably the first person to call himself an "anarchist"—have been notably clear-eyed on this matter. Even if people were entirely debased, however, this would not, as I shall argue, entail that state power is necessary or legitimate, since the people who possess this power are, contrary to some cultic approaches to state power, people, and on the whole likely to be at least as debased as everyone else. If so, handing them guns and badges might be a very bad solution to the corruption of human nature, and indeed state power has often been a much bigger problem than those it claimed to address.

III

Even were we to admit that anarchism is entirely impractical, it would not follow that it has no value. As a philosophical position, as opposed to a practical program, it is well worth entertaining—indeed it is foundational—and must be grappled with in any serious system of political philosophy. It serves the same function in political theory that skepticism serves in the theory of knowledge. Most of the great political philosophers of the modern era have taken it as a task to demonstrate that the political state is legitimate, and then to demonstrate what sort of political state is legitimate. This presupposes that an anarchist critique looms, that someone has actually challenged the legitimacy of the political state fundamentally. The weakness of these philosophers' foundational arguments—and I shall try to display this weakness elaborately in what follows—in part follows from the weakness of the critique. When, let us say, Hobbes wrote, the anarchists in England—and they were many and fundamental to the political situation Hobbes addressed—were motivated by extreme varieties of religious faith that Hobbes would have rejected out of hand as irrational. Nevertheless, perhaps because he lived during an era of civil war in which anarchists represented one extreme though central element (the "Diggers" and the "Ranters"), he displayed pervasive anxiety about the origin and legitimacy of the state. Like a lot of philosophers, he generated a kind of just-so story by which the origin of the state could be accounted for and by which its necessity and its moral legitimacy could be demonstrated. The anarchists he purported to refute, however, were no philosophers. Absolute monarchy, that is, would have a better defense if English anarchists of his era had been more philosophically articulate.

The accusation that state power rests on coercion and not on consent is something that all social contract theory understood as a fundamental challenge; it motivates the theory. If anarchism is obviously implausible, then the political works of Locke, Hobbes, and Rousseau are more or less unnecessary; they were anxious to establish that the authority of the state did not rest on mere force. This anxiety was appropriate, and a pointed critique of social contract theory from an anarchist standpoint would only have strengthened it, supposing such a critique did not refute social contract theory in a way that everyone involved would be forced to acknowledge. Anarchism, that is, is a foundational political challenge.

IV

Furthermore, anarchism, even if it is not a practical political program, can yield a sharp set of critiques of existing institutions and efforts to reform them. Since anarchism focuses intensely on whether and in what respects a given political program or institution increases or restricts freedom, it provides the sort of vigilance that can help keep us free, even in a context where anarchism itself is not seriously contemplated. Anarchism is, indeed, the only political theory that rests itself entirely on the value of freedom. Others renounce or reject freedom, or qualify it and trade it for other goods. The exclusive emphasis on freedom in anarchism might be an obsession or a derangement, and many have argued that it is. But then again only the anarchist position reveals fully whether and to what extent you are free, and to what extent you actually care whether you are free. Only an anarchist can show you that, as it happens, you don't want to be free and don't trust yourself with freedom. This is an important function especially in systems in which freedom is a great—though not the only—value, such as constitutional democracies. Anarchists within such systems are exquisitely sensitive to every respect in which institutions even in a democracy renounce their own commitment to freedom, and to the ideological claptrap with which they often conceal—even from themselves—their attacks on liberty.

One clear example of the practical function of anarchism has been its relation to Marxist communism. From the outset, in the struggles between Marx and Proudhon, this division has confronted Marxism with the truth about itself. Anarchists told Marx that "the dictatorship of the proletariat" meant merely a dictatorship of the party or an individual, and that dictatorship was wrong. It pointed out that the idea that the state, once established on a dictatorial basis, would eventually "wither away" was idiotic. The first and by far the sharpest leftist critiques of the Soviet system were made by anarchists such as Emma Goldman and Nestor Makhno, both of whom bearded Lenin in his lair even as American leftists such as John Reed were wandering the Russian countryside enthusing about the deletion of class enemies. Indeed, it is partly the decline of anarchism as a conceptual alternative that explains the credulity with which American and European leftists endorsed Stalin's regime long after its monstrousness was obvious.

V

Part of the impracticality of anarchism is a sort of conceptual defense enforced in concrete terms by state power itself. In a situation where state power more or less extends to every corner of the globe, anarchy becomes practically impossible. The state always has a tendency to confuse itself with god and to demand various forms of worship; it has achieved omnipresence, even though there are still interstices in which one might hide in the midst of various states and whole areas of life which state power does not fully saturate (though these are shrinking by the day). It moves as well toward omniscience, with ever-greater pervasion of surveillance, all of it designed to keep us safe, which is also to keep us subjected. State power thus makes itself a necessary condition of human life, which is also to say that each of us is dependent on it in various ways. No one in her right mind, I suggest, would subject herself to a state power if she lived independently of the state, but once no one lives in independence, it becomes impossible even to envision independence. The state is our horizon, the massive indubitable and inescapable fact. For an anarchist, even using the roads or buying a steak is an act of bad faith; everything is provided, supervised, inspected by the state. Its power is our dependence, and our physical dependence is one reason for our theoretical dependence; we literally cannot envision life without a state, and our inability to do so is itself an artifact of state power.

Indeed, in a situation in which political states wield atomic arsenals, tanks, artillery, automatic weapons and so on, there is no reasonable road from subjection to anarchy. The state rests ultimately on force, as of course I will argue. But force accrues to force and disqualifies all other parties from access to force. The state makes itself inevitable and makes anarchists dreamers precisely by illustrating perfectly, ever more intensely, the anarchist objection. The force the state possesses is applied to generating more force, until the idea of getting rid of the monster really is ridiculous. The state is a self-referential history, a self-reinforcing infinite spiral of oppression. Of course, the fact that state power is itself what renders state power inevitable does not show that it is not inevitable. Sadly, quite the reverse, and I expect that my children's children's children will be more thoroughly flypapered to the state than I am, should our species survive the state for a few more generations.

However, it might be worth asking after the practicality of the state itself. No doubt, states actually exist and persist, which shows them to be practical in some sense. But it is hard not to notice that the state has some practical drawbacks. The modern nation-state is an absolutely necessary condition for the wars and exterminations of the twentieth and the present century that have expended human beings as if they were inanimate. This point of view inscribes a certain irony, in that the people who administer these vast powers are themselves individual human beings. It may well be, when all is said and done, that the nation-state is responsible for the extermination of our species or the extinction of our planet. Certainly it is hard to imagine any other sort of entity developing atomic weaponry, for instance. It would be hard to hold the entity responsible for the end of all things to be practical, even if it and its effects were strictly inevitable. For the anarchist, such results are not mere epiphenomena of state power, mere unfortunate misuses of otherwise benevolent agencies, but rather a predictable outcome of the state's essence in massive fatal force.

Force, it might be said, needs no justification and brooks no refutation. Though state power avails itself of many self-justificatory practices—tales of its origins, collective festivals of loyalty—I do not deceive myself into thinking that the people who actually wield it have any serious concern about its justification. They are about the "practical business of governing," and the accompanying inspirational pomp is the advertisement of their own violence as the redemption of mankind. There is no real need for them to be political theorists, and it is very hard to imagine the average elected official or bureaucrat lying awake at night groping for the conceptual foundations of his power. The justification of state power, to those who wield it, is as impractical as the proposals for its disintegration, and of course they are right to think so, or never to think about such matters at all.

To repeat, the state need not be concerned with a general defense of its own legitimacy, though it gladly uses whatever cachet informal notions of its legitimacy may allow it to accumulate in its population. Yet it is worth thinking about what legitimacy would consist in and whether anyone ought to really be worried about it. In fact, states have no need to establish their own legitimacy in general except as a response to an anarchist critique, that is, to people who are seriously entertaining the idea that there is no obligation to obey state power. That, indeed, is the semi-practical aspect of the issue of legitimacy: it asks whether there is any binding force to authority or law that is not merely prudential. The idea that, for example, obedience to the law rests merely on prudence in the face of force could actually be, and is actually, a real threat to state power. For the notion that you have no obligation to obey the law except that it would be bad to get caught is merely an argument for not getting caught. Indeed, most people approach at least some laws in precisely this way. They've got radar detectors in their cars; they refrain from smoking their marijuana under the nose of the policeman; they commit their small crimes with a becoming discretion. Very few people have such veneration for the majesty of the law that they observe it in every aspect possible.

Even if people routinely violate the law in small ways, they also routinely accord the agents and laws of the state a variable quantum of actual respect. The actual function of the machinery by which the state celebrates its own legitimacy is to reduce its costs, which itself frees resources to increase the pervasiveness of its coercion. The state produces subjects, and part of the security and durability of any state power is the thoroughness with which it is able to do so. It produces subjects by education, by surveillance in which the subject learns to police herself, and by the pageantry of nationalism. Indeed, a key aspect of state power is aesthetic: the state seduces and awes with its architectures, its colors, its parades, even as it intimidates with its prisons and its beefy, heavily armed men. Much of the state effort that does not consist of mere force is aimed at creating the impression of this legitimacy, which is extremely expensive, but still a good investment. Although the state does not strictly need legitimacy (obviously, on my view, since it doesn't have any), it needs its people by and large more or less to behave as though it were legitimate. If it can induce this, it will take itself to be legitimate, and each person in the state apparatus can legitimize her own function.

The question of law is fundamental: what it is and what sort of obligation accrues to the status of a prescription as a law. In fact, law itself, in its "awesome majesty" and so on—law hedged around with symbols and large marble edifices—is often taken to be what distinguishes legitimate from illegitimate state power. The rule of men, the recitation goes, may well be mere rule by force; the rule of law is neutral between persons, though persons can administer it. When they do so, they do so not as individuals with the normal range of selfish interests; rather they achieve a kind of self-transcendence. So we will have to try to explore the ontological status of law: what sort of thing it is, how something of this sort can transform people into something grander than human individuals.

VI

It is unlikely that any argument could justify every sort of state power, and on any account of state power short of Hegel's, there are legitimate and illegitimate forms. Indeed, a basic purpose of the various arguments for the legitimacy of state power—which I divide in what follows into social contract, utilitarian, and justicial arguments—is to sort the legitimate from the illegitimate states. The anarchist is hence relieved also of the task of refuting every possible source and configuration of state power; we need only attack those that are most plausibly candidates for legitimacy. In my view, the democratic systems are these most plausible candidates. This is because the legitimating arguments for other systems appear to me to be much weaker, though that may be only because I am saturated by a solution of democracy, by the assertion of its exclusive legitimacy, and by the elaborate set of procedures it employs to legitimate itself. Indeed, democracy is state power legitimating itself in a situation where it has gained a bad conscience, having taken the notions of liberty and consent to be important. Democratic political theory is particularly threatened by anarchism, which claims that democracy contradicts its own goals, and claims itself to be the repository of the values democracy extols.

Furthermore, democracy relies on mechanisms to limit the extent and redress the abuses of state power; ideally it holds itself accountable to a citizenry in ways that other systems simply cannot. The milder the power of the state, the more it observes limits, the closer it approximates even my own notion of legitimacy. But it is also true that the historical march of democracy—often portrayed as the slow illumination or enlightenment of the planet—presents its own hypocrisies and puzzles. At its very base it relies on contract theory: it rests its legitimacy on the "consent of the governed." You don't have to push very hard to find immense problems with this conception. And in the fiction of consent lurks the seed of a kind of totalitarianism: there is no principled limit to political power if it is the citizen's power over herself, as Hobbes and Rousseau argued. Modern democracy is tending toward a squishy totalitarianism, in the precise sense that the democratic state pervades every aspect of every life within its borders with its regulations and bureaucracies and its projects for social amelioration, above all in its ability to produce docile citizens.

VII

Even if, again, anarchism is not a practical program, it is important as a place to stand in order to mount a critique of political philosophy and of practical politics. But I do want to suggest that anarchism has some possibilities as a practical program. Every form of human organization—including power hierarchies—that is not instituted by force is compatible with anarchist politics. And it should be said that almost all the existing forms of human organization are voluntary: the exceptions are only the political state and organized crime. Bowling leagues are anarchist organizations; no one is forced to join and no one has to be forced to obey the rules. Rather, enjoyment of the activity depends on the fact that it is rule-governed and that by and large the rules are observed. Universities have elaborate power structures, but they are

not for the most part enforced by police power. Even large companies—
though we have to go carefully here for several important reasons—for the
most part do not resort to force. If I get a job with Microsoft, I am perform-
ing my functions not because I fear being shot or imprisoned, though I may
well fear loss of my income. The last case is important, because it raises fundamental questions about whether and how voluntary association can be distinguished from involuntary, and whether specifically a ("late") capitalist economic system as a whole profoundly compromises the autonomy of those
who participate in it. What, in short, is coercion? These are questions to
which we will have to return.

Recently, internet events and approaches have provided anarchist models.
The basic ideas of open-source software and wikis (websites anyone can edit
at will) suggest that optimal orderings of tools and information, at least in
some situations, emerge through the unconstrained collaboration of many
people. Such examples have sometimes been referred to by the term *TAZ*, or
temporary autonomous zone. There is a debate within anarchism about the
value of such projects—shifting communities that evade or transcend attempts
of state and corporate powers to regulate them. However we address such
quandaries, it is perfectly clear that large cooperative efforts are possible on a
fully voluntary basis. That is actually the rule in human affairs, otherwise
human life would be unremitting slavery. Even the activities of the state itself
consist to some extent of cooperative enterprises in which people engage
through incentive or even enthusiasm. Indeed, it is possible to think that the
good works of the state, of which there are many, are unnecessarily sullied by
the fact that underlying the cooperation are people with guns willing to
enforce the tax code and a sprawling system of incarceration. Some anarchists
may have an unwarrantedly positive view of "human nature," but its opposite
is surely a dark view: that people could not voluntarily create roads, put out
fires, and perform many of the reasonable tasks performed by the state under
the auspices of forced taxation. The latter claim is belied by many cooperative
enterprises in which people are engaged all the time without being threatened
with detention should they withdraw.

The practical question then might be: to what extent are voluntary
arrangements of the sort we are all engaged in a possible source for the necessary or positive functions of the state? This is a difficult question, and one that
we have no real prospect of examining by practical experiment for the reasons
just alluded to. The contrast of a bowling league or a university to a state may
not be fair or useful. On the other hand, it shows by contrast clearly that whatever it might say about itself the state does rest on force.

VIII

Communism and democracy, among other political ideas, have incredibly elaborate philosophical rationalizations. They have their grand systematizers as well as their world-historical figures. This is not quite true of anarchism, where both the theory and practice are a bit spotty. One should expect no more of anarchists, I suppose. Still, I feel that there are still some theoretical moves to be made, whereas in some of the other cases essentially all the work has been done. (Fascism, too, has flimsy theoretical underpinnings; let's keep it that way.) This is not to say that no anarchist political philosopher has done serious or systematic work. I would in particular point to Peter Kropotkin and Lysander Spooner on different poles of anarchist theory. But even some of the best-known anarchist theoreticians are inconsistent or just a big mess: Proudhon and Bakunin spring to mind. Others have been more activists or revolutionaries than theoreticians, and this is true even of Emma Goldman, who was not a particularly original figure as regards her anarchism.

As several great anarchists—most clearly Voltairine de Cleyre—have pointed out, there can be no political philosophy of anarchism, if by that is meant a detailed prescription for how people will arrange their lives once those lives are free of coercion. A detailed blueprint of the future is what we might call an "ideology." Marxist communism is the most famous example, but any system that starts with a utopia—Plato's, for instance, or even the ideal democracies envisioned by Locke or Madison—are ideological in this sense. But the ideological impulse is a totalitarian impulse, an attempt to impose one's will on future persons. Because I myself focus in my political writing so much on the destruction of existing institutions and so little on positive programs for amelioration of the world's ills, my position is often dismissed as useless. And this very tendency is one reason that anarchism is associated with mindless destruction. But anarchism is mindful destruction. It is precisely its refusal to shape and impose a future that distinguishes anarchism from ideologies; we want to let people go, and see what happens. In an existential or cosmic sense, I would say, that is the actual situation: we've been let go down here, and what is happening is happening. It's precisely in the attempt to seize control of the future that we have been about the busy work of destroying one another.

All of this is not to say that there cannot, in another sense, be a philosophy of anarchism that is as deep as any political philosophy. A philosophy of anarchism can begin in an ontology and a cosmology: in a sense of what the universe is and how it is ordered. It can proceed to an understanding of what it means to be human. It can entail and be entailed by a system of values: aesthetic, ethical, and epistemic. In a certain way, I think every political philosophy is a ramification of and ramifies into all of these dimensions of understanding, and there is no reason for anarchism to be any less profound or systematic in these respects than the political philosophy of Plato, or Augustine, or Marx.

Anarchism is more vital now than at any time since the early twentieth century. Punk rockers and antiglobalization activists, squatters and drifters, small farmers and freaks around the world, have taken to calling themselves anarchists. The scrawled red circle *A* is one of the world's most ubiquitous graffiti. The current anarchist revival too is a bit underfed philosophically, though it draws strongly on the work of such figures as Noam Chomsky, John Zerzan, Alan Moore, and Hakim Bey. And perhaps, as many younger anarchists would insist, philosophical system is neither necessary nor desirable. But if anarchism is one of my derangements, philosophy is another, and so I'm going to give you a dose whether you want it or not. And if you refuse to read this book, I will stun-gun you, cuff you, and lock you in my basement.

IX

Here is an outline of my argument in this book. First, I try to define some key terms, including *anarchism, freedom, coercion,* and *state.* Then I consider the dominant justifications of state power. I consider them, as they must be considered, as responses to an anarchist challenge. I sort the justifications of state power into social contract theories, utilitarian theories, and justicial theories (*justicial* sounds like a pidgin coinage, but it's in the OED). I try to show, first, that each of these is unsound, for reasons that more or less will apply to any example of a theory of that type. I conclude from the flimsiness and inconsistency of these arguments that state power cannot be shown to be legitimate, though of course it is always possible that some theory may arise which does a better job than the traditional ones. The notion that the state is legitimate is equivalent to the notion that the state should exist. So if all theories that legitimize state power were false, that would show that it's not the case that state should exist. The task of this book, then, is wholly negative and destructive: it's the black bomb that, as an anarchist, I habitually carry around.

I intend to frame a positive anarchist philosophy in another book, and I associate my own brand of anarchism with the American individualism of Ralph Waldo Emerson, William Lloyd Garrison, Henry David Thoreau, and Josiah Warren. This tradition is distinct from the egoism of Max Stirner and the hypercapitalistism of Ayn Rand, and it is also distinct from the communist anarchism of Mikhail Bakunin and Emma Goldman. It calls for nonexploitive cooperative economies and affirms the possibilities of love and generosity between individuals. Its basic political commitment is what Warren called "self-sovereignty," an idea that developed out of two interlocked sources: the Protestant Reformation in its radical aspects and the American abolitionist movement. The former entailed liberty of conscience: it left to each person that person's relation to god, and it made individual conscience the only legitimate regulator of human action. The latter had sudden radical entailments: if no one could legitimately own another, then each person was the owner of herself. At its most metaphysical, the tradition with which I associate myself makes the apparently paradoxical claims that individuals are sovereign over themselves and that individuals consist of their relations: to other human beings, to the natural world, and to god (if any). This metaphysics of the individual in the universe is an image of an ideal political situation. I conclude this book with an outline intended to give a sense of where these ideas will end up taking us.

chapter one

some definitions

I

Anarchism, as I am using the term here, refers to the view that all forms of human association ought to be voluntary. If it is true, as against some varieties of social contract theory, that what is known as the political state is not a voluntary association but in fact rests on coercion and is destructive or limiting of the liberties of its subjects, then anarchism in my sense entails that the political state is never legitimate or, as I will put it equivalently, that state power is not morally justified. This leaves us with a number of key terms to define before we go forward: *voluntary, state, coercion, legitimacy*. A number of other terms arise in the task of defining or understanding those, including *sovereignty, nation, person*, and others. Several of these terms are among the most contentious in philosophy, law, and elsewhere, and a full-dress project of defining them cannot be assayed here. But in many cases a justification of state power, or of a certain form of state power, would follow very quickly from certain ways of defining these terms. Indeed, parts my own position are going to fall like ripe fruit from the tree of meaning, so I want to defend some of the characterizations I give of the meanings of these terms as relatively neutral, commonsensical, or in line with the way the terms are used in ordinary language.

II

The terms *freedom* and *liberty* are used more or less interchangeably in what follows, though I tend to prefer the term *liberty* as being central to an American anti-authoritarian tradition with which I associate myself. Notoriously, both terms are used in many senses. As F.A. Hayek has pointed out, they have two primary (and related) uses in political contexts: the absence of restraints imposed by others and scope for action in the social sphere. The first is sometimes called "negative" and the latter "positive" freedom. In the first sense, which is the primary meaning of the term in what follows, *liberty* is interdefined with *coercion*. Hayek: "['Liberty' or 'freedom' originally meant] always the possibility of a person's acting according to his own decisions and plans, in contrast to the position of one who was irrevocably subject to the will of another, who by arbitrary decision could coerce him to act or not to act in specific ways. . . . In this sense 'freedom' refers solely to a relation of men to other men, and the only infringement on it is coercion by men."[1] I do not intend to put any weight on the idea that this is the "original" meaning of the terms *liberty* and *freedom*, but it is the primary sense in which I will use these terms in this book. To be a free person in this sense is to be opposed to being a slave; or it is to be the owner of oneself in the sense that one is not subject to the will of another except by one's choice to be so. It encompasses freedoms such as being free of arbitrary imprisonment, being free to move or travel, being free to speak as one wills, and so on. Freedom, in short, is self-sovereignty, which is to be opposed to being owned by others, in whatever degree or respect.

Here in somewhat more detail is Hayek on coercion:

> By 'coercion' we mean such control of the environment or circumstances of a person by another that, in order to avoid greater evil, he is forced to act not according to a coherent plan of his own but to serve the ends of another. Except in the sense of choosing the lesser evil in a situation forced on him by another, he is unable to use his own intelligence or knowledge or to follow his own aims and beliefs. Coercion is evil precisely because it thus eliminates an individual as a thinking and valuing person and makes him a bare tool in the achievement of the ends of another. (Hayek, pp. 20, 21)

Such a characterization has the advantages of being relatively familiar in our experience and of not immediately raising impossible metaphysical questions. By *liberty*, of course, I do not mean free will in the context of a deterministic or law-governed universe, nor the power to do whatever one likes, but simply the condition of being fundamentally autonomous from the sheer will of others, of being in a position in which, if someone barks an order at you or for that matter gently hints that you might want to pursue a particular course of action, the costs of disobedience are not catastrophic. In most cases, coercion does not merely make alternative courses of action impossible, or literally operate your body like a marionette; it proceeds by punishing disobedience. In the very clearest cases, you can demur, but you will pay with your life. To choose to obey the will of another person in order to preserve your life is, as I will use the term here, to be coerced. The means by which the person who commands obedience as a condition of your continued life or well-being bends you to his will is force.

Coercion is of course a matter of degree, and we might just try to enumerate some cases and ponder them as illustrating degrees of coercion. For example: If you don't do what I'm telling you to do, (1) I will kill you; (2) I will kill someone else; (3) I will imprison you; (4) I will imprison someone else; (5) I will take away your livelihood; (6) I will injure you; (7) I will fine you or take some of your possessions; (8) I will limit your future prospects; (9) I will whine until your life is sheer misery, and so on. Whatever the definition, there will be a range of difficult cases in which we are not certain whether or to what extent to characterize a certain situation as coercive, and hence whether or to what extent to characterize a choice as free. Although we will have to deal with some puzzles, it will be enough to proceed if the reader will recognize that there are certain clear cases, and if the reader is not enthusiastic about being the coerced party in such situations. Some sorts of coercion on some occasions are obviously egregious and others are relatively mild. Insofar as they are indeed cases of coercion, they all carry with them the presumption that they must be justified.

A paradigmatic case of coercion would be blackmail, wherein I limit your choice situation in a way intended to benefit myself by imposing massive costs on the act of refusal. The higher these costs, as you understand them, the more coerced is your choice to submit to my wishes. In short, where your choice situation is delimited for my purposes by the imposition of high costs on alternatives to the course of action that I propose for you, there is coercion.

There is another range of cases, however, in which the range of actions is limited by means that are not as direct as the threat of force or the leverage provided by blackmail. Consider, for example, cases in which someone else controls one's access to information and insulates one from information that could have led one to behave differently. This could be a direct series of lies, for example, together with restrictions on research and communication that could be expected to lead to an exposure of those lies. Even in cases where there is no question of large-scale censorship or of penalties for free expression, the attempt to deceive people or restrict their access to information is an attempt to delimit their choice situation, and is hence closely related to coercion. Where a censorship regime is backed by armed force, of course, it is coercion in the proper sense. And there may be much more elaborate technologies of coercion, which will also produce difficult cases.

What I have in mind are the sorts of cases investigated most sharply by Michel Foucault, in which institutions are actually dedicated to shaping the consciousness of people who fall into their ambit, as in some prisons, schools, and military units, for example. Here the perfectly clear cases might involve secret administration of drugs or hypnosis and so on, though the ordinary processes in modernity by which people come to know or believe that they are always under surveillance may be extremely difficult to adjudicate as coercive or noncoercive. One function of such institutions is to conceal or even actually to avoid coercion. Perhaps *coercion* is sometimes the wrong term here, and the people who invent such technologies of the human often specifically contrast them to coercive or police techniques. And yet in some ways these practices are more central to the operation of state and other sorts of power than direct threats of violence or imprisonment. And there could perhaps (though perhaps not) be states that dispense with direct coercion completely and rest content with manufacturing docile personalities.

Such measures, which are more and more pervasive as strategies of state authority but also exist in corporations and other organizations, are typically backed with some threat. But as they are perfected and as the technologies by which they are accomplished become more developed, such threats may become less and less necessary, or they may become more and more shrouded by layers of obscuring institutional activity. What such cases have in common with classical coercion, however, is that the scope of choice is limited by the intentional action of human beings. It is a nice question whether such techniques are preferable to plain, old-fashioned coercion as being less violent and deadly or whether they are scarier and more insidious (because more difficult to resist). But I would start with the same inquiry: would you be satisfied to put the formation of your personality in the hands of some person or group of persons, or would you regard this as a violation of your freedom? Do you acknowledge the right of any person to re-make you into a more normal or cooperative person without your explicit consent?

Hayek's definition seems somewhat too tight if it excludes as coercion the effects of surveillance backed with punishment. But it is also too loose if one takes him to mean that any situation in which one chooses the lesser of two evils in a choice situation partly defined by another person is coercive. Where the price of disobedience or dissent is not astronomical, the choice can be relatively free. This shows among other things that freedom in the present sense is a matter of degree, from being a meat puppet to being entirely unconstrained by other persons. Very typical and decent human interactions shape choice situations in noncoercive ways. You know, for example, that if you act like that, I will get angry. This imposes a cost on the behavior but in the typical case is not coercive unless my anger carries with it the threat of considerable harm.

Nor do I necessarily want to import Hayek's antipathy to freedom construed "positively" as power within all the world to do what one likes. For example, it is often argued that people who are starving are not free, though they may not be specifically constrained by other persons (in a large-scale famine for example) or, more widely, that poor people are unfree no matter what the origin of their poverty. These are reasonable uses of the term *freedom* and are continuous with ("negative") freedom from the will of other people. In many cases, it is impossible to determine whether the scope of one's actions is constrained primarily by the will of others or not, as in cases of large-scale exploitative economies in which one's prospects are severely limited, while those of others are massively opened up, by a set of economic arrangements or institutions. Even if one merely contrasts freedom to slavery, such cases can be obscure. So let me say that freedom from the arbitrary will of another is a necessary condition of freedom in its wider senses and may in some ways be continuous with it. I shall be primarily concerned here with freedom in Hayek's sense. Freedom in this sense is, of course, primarily what is at issue in political philosophy. And the desirability of freedom in this sense is almost universally affirmed, at least among contemporary political thinkers.

III

There are various ways to say why there should be this agreement. One would be the intuitive pull of the concept of natural rights, even among those who do not accept the doctrine or do not see how it could be defended. Let me put it like this: there can hardly be a person who would simply acknowledge that they themselves could legitimately be enslaved. Whatever your notion of rights, I hope that you feel that there ought to be some zone of autonomy around yourself, and that when you yourself are used as a mere tool or device of some other person, some important principle or reality is being violated or denied. At a minimum, in order to suggest that someone ought to be enslaved, a rational argument would be required to show that there is some quality of the slave or of the master or in the overwhelming force of circumstances that would justify enslavement. Of course, people have given many such accounts: blackness of skin, irrationality, femaleness, or Jewish ancestry, for example. These views can hardly have many contemporary proponents, but in any case the matter ought to rest on what the prospective slave would think about the relevant justification.

In other words, if you would not endorse your own complete subjection to the will of another person, I think you ought to extend your argument to any other person. If you do not, then I want to know on what substantive grounds you do not, and then I will quarrel with those grounds. I would appreciate it if, unlike the enthusiasts of slavery down through the ages, you don't merely say that people like you should be allowed to coerce people like them, for your or their own good. An argument like that really ought to carry with it a burden of proof because of its transparently self-serving quality. I would like to see an argument in favor of slavery made by the sort of person who will end up enslaved if the argument wins the day; one rarely hears this, and if one does, one must suspect that the statement is itself coerced. But in the absence of such an argument, I will simply assert and assume that subjection to the arbitrary will of another is never legitimate.

In every case milder than this, there must be some argument that tends to show that subjection of that kind, or to that degree, or with regard to this particular range of actions, is legitimate. I want the burden of proof on the assertion that a person can legitimately be coerced. There are, of course, many possible arguments and many possible cases. Perhaps one can be coerced in some fairly mild ways in order to achieve some set of benefits to oneself or to others. Perhaps one can be coerced in some ways in virtue of reduced agency in oneself, as in cases of addiction. Perhaps one can be subjected to coercion in order to save one's own life or the lives of others, or to give others certain opportunities, or to achieve a higher degree of equality in various other ways. I simply want to insist, however, that some such argument must be given, because there is a presumption against coercion, which might alternately be formulated as saying that there is a close to universal aspiration to freedom from the will of others. Of course, state power plausibly involves coercion of some persons by others, and hence in any given case must be justified by some argument or other, on pain of slavery.

IV

That's all. That's the rigorous foundation of ethics on which my political philosophy rests: the ability to take up the point of view of a person subject to the arbitrary will of another. I leave it to the reader to determine whether this is Kantianism, utilitarianism, emotivism, or the merest irrationalism. At any rate, I can envision a more systematic political ethics, but I cannot imagine a more convincing one, and that will be quite enough to be getting along with. I suppose the universality I am attributing to the intuition that one does not want to be subjected might be the merest artifact of centuries of liberal individualism. In the golden age there were communities wherein the people were enthusiastic about their subjection, or were incapable of distinguishing their will from the will of the theocracy. Yes, only, no. The extent to which every single hierarchy of which we have any knowledge generates its skeptics, gadflies, and rebels. must never be left unappreciated, even if that extent is hard to reconstruct, because the people who express it and their expressions of it traditionally have been immolated.

V

Voluntary in the definition of anarchism above means, simply, uncoerced. As coercion is a matter of degree, so is voluntariness. Anarchism in this sense means that more voluntary arrangements are always preferable, other things being equal, to less voluntary ones. Notice that this does not entail that coercion can never be justified or that the ultimate moral fact is the autonomy of persons. The present position is compatible with a utilitarian or other justification of coercion in some particular case.

Free action is voluntary action, and political freedom or liberty is the overall condition of a life over a segment of time in which one is not subject to coercion by political or state authorities, or is subject to coercion only to some limited extent.

Hence these terms are interdefinable. Anarchism is the view that all forms of human association ought to be voluntary, or it is the view that people ought to have maximal political freedom. This will entail, I think, that there ought to be no government.

VI

The term *state*, which seems so clear in its basic uses, is remarkably slippery. Is it, for example, a group of people? a set of institutions? Neither seems promising, in that the people or institutions can be entirely transformed while the state remains the same state it was; this is more or less true of most modern states. Often the state is defined in terms of its sovereign power, which is in turn defined as the legitimate use of force or the power to enforce the laws. This will not suffice in the present context, because it would beg all the relevant questions; of course if the state is characterized as legitimate sovereignty, anarchism is false. The anarchist could then, in this quibbling about terms, simply argue that there are no actual states; that is, there are no legitimate sovereign powers. But this seems perverse both ways around.

The state at a first stab ought to be distinguished from the nation, which roughly indicates a large geographical area and the people therein, in their aspect as having a "shared identity." But even here there are counter-examples, as in diasporic nations. Consider, for example, "black nationalism," in which a common identity, emerging from a common history, is asserted, but in which the territory, if any, is scattered or yet-to-be-occupied, or is an aspiration. It may be, though, that the territoriality referred to is primarily a common origin point in Africa, and nationalism the imagination of a return.

It is certain that the conditions of identity placed on nations are different from those placed on states. For example the nation of Kurdistan extends over parts of Turkey, Syria, Iraq, and Iran. But in all these cases territoriality is relevant, even if imaginary. We might sum up nationality as an identity, possibly encompassing shared language, history, ethnicity, or race, anchored in imagination in a shared place. What a national identity is, and whether it corresponds to something real or manufactures something real, are questions we need not belabor. We can also hold in abeyance the question of whether nationality is desirable. It is foundationally aesthetic, and relies on symbol systems, songs, monuments, literatures, and so on. What is important to notice is that states do not coincide neatly with nations, though the two are related and though states use or crystallize national identities in their struggle for legitimacy, or to assert a claim to loyalty. Anarchists could be opposed to nations in this sense, or be skeptics about their real existence, but they need not be.

In fact, states and nations in modernity are symbiotic; states invent nations, or they forge and enforce and extend them. States use nations as means of asserting legitimacy, and hence encourage the identities that go with them, though they probably also try to expunge rival identities. Nations enter into and leave states, extend across their borders and then are reincorporated, declare their independence and then enforce an account of their identity. So one does not simply want to make the nation natural and the state artificial, the nation primordial and the state parasitic; they use each other and oscillate in and out of identity.

VII

We probably ought to distinguish between the meaning of *state* and the meaning of *government*. The latter, of course, sounds like the name of a process, the process of "governing." The government consists of the set of persons who are doing the governing, the tools, and perhaps the procedures by which they do so: the people who are controlling certain aspects of behavior by certain rules, or who are channeling the lives of people within a given territory in certain ways, and the means by which they accomplish this task. Government is specifically territorial, as in county governments, state governments, and (even) national governments; where there is a national government, the nation is territorialized.

I think that any way you look at it, there can be no government that does not possess and employ coercive force in a fairly pervasive way over a certain territory. This is, I suggest, necessary and sufficient, and there is no conceptual requirement of legitimacy, or justfiedness, or consent, or anything else. Think about how you would actually use the word *government* in certain cases.

Let's say you discovered an island where the people wearing yellow shirts post lists of rules. When members of the larger group of people in blue shirts are caught by people in yellow shirts violating the list of rules, they are pistol-whipped and thrown in a dungeon. The Yellow Ones possess a large cache of weapons, and if a Blue One is caught with a weapon, it is confiscated. The Yellow Ones pay for the enforcement of their rules by demanding a tribute; if you fail to pay you are pistol-whipped and thrown into a dungeon. This tribute money accounts for the fact that the Yellow Ones live in comparative luxury and labor comparatively little. Now, as you land on this island in your exploration of the terrestrial globe, would you be in any doubt about who constituted the island's government? If the Yellow Ones were elected by the people in blue shirts, the Yellow Ones constitute the government. If the Great God Yottle selected them, they are the government. If they rule with a benevolent hand, they are the government. And if they have not a shred of any sort of consent or divine approbation, if they are entirely arbitrary and vicious, they are still— to precisely the same extent—the government of the island.

At the municipal hut there is a vitrine in which rests a document establishing the Rule of the Yellow Ones, signed by every person on the island. Or in the basement of the municipal hut there is a dungeon which houses a hostage from every one of the island's families; the disobedience of any member of any family is punished by the hostage's death. Either way, if you want to negotiate a treaty or purchase part of the island, you will go to the Yellow Ones.

On the other hand, let's say the Blue Ones post a list of rules, but have no ability to enforce them at all. In fact, whenever they try, they are pistol-whipped and thrown in dungeons. However, in a vitrine in the municipal hut there is a document ordaining the rule of the Blue Ones forever and unto eternity, signed by etc. If you're trying to figure out who runs the island, this document is worthless. Necessary and sufficient.

Institutions other than governments exercise power by coercion; indeed most institutions of any size have some coercive component. For example, schools, whether or not they are government-run, maintain discipline by a schedule of punishments. Corporations punish dissenters or unproductive employees with the withdrawal of their livelihoods, and so on. One thing to notice is that coercion in such contexts usually does not have a substrate of violence. That is, Wal-Mart can fire you, but if they shoot you they will be subject to legal sanction, and if you steal from them they will bring police with guns and cells into the picture; if force is required, they will call upon the state. Of course there may also be some degree of force, for example corporal punishment in parochial schools, underlying coercion in some of these cases. Again the concepts are slippery, and if I called a school that relied heavily on pedagogical beatings a "dictatorship," you would understand me. But one feature that makes government distinctive, it seems to me, is that though it may deploy many styles and strategies of coercion, they are erected on a substructure of death: the state, if nothing else, arrogates to itself the right to use deadly force.

It may also be that the government permits or ignores force or violence by certain persons at certain times, for example (traditionally) husbands against their wives, parents against their children, teachers against their pupils. It would not be quite right to say that the state authorizes this coercion, but it does permit it, which is often necessary for it to continue. This can be seen by the fact that should sufficient motivations arise, the government can intervene in these relationships. Many governments do so continuously.

At one time almost all governments imposed death sentences for some offenses; now, many do not. But the agents of the government, the bottom-line enforcement agencies, have access to deadly force. They are both armed and authorized in the use of arms in enforcement. Typically, as well, the government is uniquely the prosecutor of war, which always involves attributing to its own agents the right to kill. The military structures that almost invariably accompany governments also have the effect of implying that ultimately, internal rebellion is useless in that it can be crushed with overwhelming deadly force.

It may be that government could replace deadly force with other techniques, and it may be that this is already in process. Universal surveillance, control of media, and control of educational and medical systems already do largely displace deadly force as governing strategies. All of these are coercive in the sense that they delimit choice situations for the sake of goals external to the individual agent. The bottom line, however, is still deadly force, and it must be appealed to when the other strategies fail. It is hard to imagine a situation in which deadly force could be dispensed with entirely; no government has come anywhere close to doing so. For one thing, government must be mobilized to some extent to resist invasion. Perhaps there may eventually be a single world government that can dispense with deadly force entirely and depend on other forms of coercive control. In such circumstances, the definition of *government* would have to be revised. A rather horrendous fact is that such a situation might be highly desirable on utilitarian grounds. It would not, of course, follow that it was a good situation. In fact, it is possible already to become nostalgic for force, with its primitive directness, its honesty, its . . . innocence.

I define *government* as follows: a government is a group of people who claim and, to an effective extent, exercise a monopoly of coercion resting on deadly force over a definite geographical area and the artifacts and procedures by which they do so. Of course this monopoly is never complete, and the government may even authorize some people not part of itself to exercise coercion in some cases, such as in a scheme to privatize the prison system. It may in fact permit violence in various other cases. These authorizations and permissions themselves suppose and make use of the government's monopoly of coercion. Being a government on this conception requires that the effectiveness of the monopoly on coercion reach a certain (unspecified) threshold before the group exercising it has a claim to be a government. Notice that to the extent that the government or the former government loses this monopoly, the nation or public is plunged into a condition of anarchy or is precipitated into or generates a new state. By the same token, when any group effectively exercises such a monopoly, when the LAPD won't venture into the Crips' territory, for example, that group becomes the government of that territory (and indeed in the imagined case is likely to start up a system of taxation, social services, and so on).

By 'artifacts' I refer to weapons, vehicles, buildings, papers, computers, and so on. Indeed, a monopoly of force is close to impossible without the use of, at a minimum, weapons. Government originates in technologies by which coercion is, as we say, implemented. Here I do not want to focus exclusively on the actual technologies of death, though these have, under government auspices, been brought to a peak of annihilating effectiveness that they could never have reached otherwise. Understand: on my view, the fact that we owe to governments the amazing technologies of death which confront us is not a coincidence. It is government expressing its essence in the processes of history, unfurling its flag over a period of millennia. But there are other functions that the monopoly of deadly force performs that may in part motivate it; I have in mind particularly commercial and religious functions, above all the function of keeping definitive or authoritative records. If government deserves discredit for death, it may also deserve credit for extreme refinement of linguistic and mathematical techniques and technologies. Here again, however, the direction may be totality—a government capable of total surveillance.

Under 'procedures' I would include the hierarchical arrangement of officials, again brought to mind-numbing elaboration by the time our species achieves its true happy flowering in bureaucracy. 'Procedures' might also be taken to include the rules and regulations by which they operate insofar as these are summaries of the actual actions of persons (rather than mere claptrap). Procedures include, above all, mechanical forms of human action, habit frozen into the continuous action of millions of people over generations, a form of compulsion by which the same structure of behavior is instantiated again and again and again.

VIII

A number of thinkers, including, classically, the great libertarian Randolph Bourne and, more recently, the military historian Martin Creveld, have characterized the state as "abstract." Creveld writes:

> The state, then, is an *abstract* entity which can neither be seen, nor heard, nor touched. This entity is not identical with either the rulers or the ruled; neither President Clinton, nor citizen Smith, nor even an assembly of all the citizens acting in common can claim that they *are* the state. . . . This is as much to say that the state . . . is a corporation, just as universities, trade unions, and churches *inter alia* are. . . . Above all, it is a corporation in the sense that it possesses a legal *persona* of its own, which means that it has rights and duties and may engage in various activities *as if* it were a real, flesh-and-blood, living individual. The points where the state differs from other corporations are, first, the fact that it authorizes them all but is itself authorized (recognized) solely by others of its kind; secondly, that certain functions (known collectively as the attributes of sovereignty) are reserved for it alone; and, thirdly, that it exercises those functions over a certain territory inside which its jurisdiction is both exclusive and all-embracing.[2]

One way into the history of this idea is provided by Bertrand de Jouvenel: the state evolves as a machinery for executing the will of one man. Subtract this one man and it still behaves, or at least is interpreted as behaving, as a single will or agent.

> The apparatus of the state is built by and for personal power.
>
> For the will of one man alone to be transmitted and exercised throughout a wide kingdom, transmission and execution must both be systematized and given the means of growth—in other words, bureaucracy, police, taxation. For monarchy this state apparatus is the natural and necessary instrument. But on society too, its influence down the centuries is so great that, when at long last the monarch has vanished without disturbing it, its motive power will still be conceived of only as one will, though it is now the will of an abstract person who has taken the monarch's place. The mind's eye will see, for instance, the nation deciding and the apparatus of state executing its decisions.[3]

There are many forms of this attribution of will to an abstract person or to a bureaucracy: the Hobbes Leviathan, Rousseau's general will, and so on. And its quasi-deification, necessary to legitimate its power, is found all over the origins of the concept. The chief is the descendant of a god; the emperor is the embodiment of a god; the king rules by divine will. Go to Washington, D.C., and enter the temples in which the state is worshiped, literally based on the temple architecture of Greece and Rome. It is easy, but for all that necessary, to ridicule these pretensions, for they are ridiculous, and I will baste them in their own juices in what follows. But for now it is necessary merely to grasp the ontology: state as abstract or figurative or fictional agent.

The state is in particular the agent of life and death, and it is this power of the state that surely accounts for its promotion to divine status. What can kill you or dispossess you on a whim is surely more or less a god, call it what you like. It consists in sheer power as well as its mystifications and obscurities; the state's ceremonies and its implacable, irresistible decrees preserve for us, as for the ancients, our feeling deep inside that the state deserves our worship, that we ought to erase our will before it. Everyone more or less feels the same, from patriotic veterans to welfare-state liberals.

If a nation is the identity of a people, a state is the identity of a government. The treaty case, as Creveld insists, is central because the state is centrally defined as one among a group of states, competent to act as a person in its dealings with other states. The state is one variety of corporation, and this is precisely how it is treated conceptually in its modern origins. For a government to be represented as a state, there must be someone that speaks for this government or some way that this government speaks and renders decisions. Or a host of ways, as long as it is "the state" that is the agent of these actions. In other words, the state is the imaginary or abstract agent of the acts of a government, and the acts of the government, by definition, implicate coercive force.

The classical statement of this account of the state is made at the moment of the maturity of the modern European state, the moment of its liberation from the fetters of empire and church, by Hobbes in *Leviathan*. (The modern "nation-state" is often dated to the Peace of Westphalia, 1648; *Leviathan* was published in 1651.)

> A PERSON is he *whose words or actions are considered, either as his own, or as representing the words or actions of another man, or of any other thing to whom they are attributed, whether Truly or by Fiction.*
>
> When they are considered as his own, then is he called a *Naturall Person*: and when they are considered as representing the words and actions of another, then is he a *Feigned* or *Artificiall person.*
>
> The word person is Latin, instead whereof the Greeks have *prosopon*, which signifies the *Face*, as *persona* in latine signifies the *disguise*, or *outward appearance* of a man, counterfeited on the Stage; and sometimes more particularly that part of it which disguiseth the face, as a *Mask* or *Visard*: and from the stage hath been translated to any Representer of speech and action, as well in Tribunalls as Theatres. So that a *Person* is the same that an *Actor* is, both on the stage and in common Conversation; and to *Personate* is to *Act* or *Represent* himselfe, or an other; and he that acteth another is said to beare his Person, or act in his name (in which sense *Cicero* useth it where he says, *Unus sustineo tres Personas; Mei, Adversarii, et Judicis*—I bear three Persons; my own, my Adversaries, and the Judges), and is called in diverse occasions, diversely; as a *Representer*, or *Representative*, a *Lieutenant*, a *Vicar*, an *Attorney*, a *Deputy*, a *Procurator*, an *Actor*, and the like.[4]

He then defines a commonwealth: "One person, of whose Acts a great Multitude, by mutuall Covenants one with another, have made themselves every one the Author, to the end he may use the strength and means of them all as he shall think expedient for their Peace and Common Defence" (Hobbes, p. 228). A state, reinterpreting this slightly, is an abstract person who represents the people and embodies the combined deadly force of them all.

To actually define the state as "bearing the person" of all the people, however, would be to beg the question in favor of social contract theory, which is radically false. At a minimum it is obvious that the state does not conceptually require universal consent, but only the consent of those within it who actually operate or can appeal to its mechanisms of violence. This is as obvious in Hobbes's philosophy as anywhere, even as he apparently appeals to universal consent. All social contract theorists, as we shall see, appeal to universal consent in the first move, then dump it overboard as explicitly as possible in the second. At any rate, it is obvious that actual states have existed without this sort of consent and that no state has ever existed that had it; consent is simply not criterial of statehood. So ask yourself: who is being "personated"?

At any rate, I will for the most part use *state* and *government* interchangeably: a state is a representation of the actual scattered group of people, buildings, weapons, hard drives, and so on that are parts of the government and that do the work of governing. The state is an external representation—the imaginary entity with which other states deal—and it is an internal representation—the government as embodied in a single phrase, as in "The United Kingdom" or "The Democratic Republic of the Congo." It is a personification and a name for the government. It is a "flag" one might say; when American children pledge allegiance to the flag, they are pledging allegiance to the state in a spiral of representations. The representational status and practices of the state are used as strategies of government; they make the state elusive, apparently separate it from any specific persons, and suggest gently that the state has transcended the mundane plane of existence. This in turn helps make possible the cult of the state as captured in whole swathes of political philosophy and everyday practices. We will try to make our way through the dogmas of this cult in what follows, even as we attempt to deflect or destroy its zombie acolytes.

Notice, however, that there are forms of government that are not represented as states: Empires, for instance, in which the style of representation is entirely different; the empire is essentially represented by the adorned body of the emperor. Obviously, the power of an empire also requires coercion, and an empire can only originate in conquest. If anarchism is the view that human relations ought to be voluntary, that is, uncoerced, it is also incompatible with empires, certain varieties of tribal chieftainships, and so on. Some of the arguments against the legitimacy of state power that follow will apply *mutatis mutandis* to these other governmental forms. Nevertheless, it is as against the modern nation-state that anarchism developed as a political philosophy and toward which its antipathy is most directed.

It is widely held that the state is in decline. In the work of Habermas and many others, this is chalked up to the "globalization" of the economy and information networks. It is held that these developments make transnational government inevitable; the EU is commonly provided as an example of the new layers of bureaucracy that will someday befuddle and feed us all. I have no idea whether this is the case, and I do want to mention that the globalization

of the economy has also been accompanied by an explosion of intense nation-
alisms, religious sectarianisms, and other counter-movements. The local may
prove hard to eradicate. But as the arguments below will for the most part
count against empires, they will for the most part count against whatever comes
next, until such time as everyone pays taxes enthusiastically.

IX

To say of a state that it is legitimate is, on my construal, to say that its use of
coercion is morally justifiable. Alternatively, it is to say that the laws it enforces
are coercible—that it is morally legitimate to enforce them—and that one has
a prima facie duty to obey persons acting in their capacity as authorized agents
of the state. This I believe is in keeping with the use of these terms in the lit-
erature by those who do believe that state power can be shown in some cases
to be legitimate. At a minimum, it seems to me that an adequate argument for
state legitimacy must entail these results. If specifically coercion by the state
cannot be justified morally, whatever is left legitimate is compatible with anarchy. That is, if it were true, as some philosophers have momentarily fantasized,
that the state is or could be a fully voluntary association, then the state is an
anarchistic organization. We can now dispose of or clarify the idea that the state
is a body that exercises sovereignty: if *sovereignty* is defined as the morally justified monopoly of coercion resting on deadly force, then to define states as having it begs the anarchist question. But since we call things "states" or "governments" without regard to their legitimacy, we cannot in keeping with the
ordinary meaning of the terms include sovereignty, unless that just means the
monopoly of force.

X

Summary of definitions:

Anarchism: the political philosophy according to which all human associations
ought to be fully voluntary.

Coercion: limitation of a choice situation faced by a person P by the intentional
act of Q, for Q's purposes; typically constraint to a certain course of action by
increasing the costs of the alternatives.

Voluntary: uncoerced.

Force: the means by which the person who commands obedience as a condition of your continued life or well-being bends you to his will.

Political freedom or *liberty*: the condition of a life over a segment of time in which one is not subject to coercion by government, or is subject to coercion by government only to some limited extent.

Government: a group of people who claim and to an effective extent exercise a monopoly of coercion, resting on deadly force, over a definite geographical area, and the artifacts and procedures by which they do so.

State: the corporate agent of the acts of a government; the representation of a government as a singular actor.

Legitimacy: the quality of a state in virtue of which its coercive force is morally justifiable, or in virtue of which its laws impose prima facie duties.

Sovereignty: legitimate governing power; coercive control over territory and the persons therein by a legitimate government.

XI

Besides a clarification of terms, there are two things that I would like to take from this chapter into the rest of the book. First, the state is in its essence an arrangement of coercions. And second, coercion must always be justified and is always prima facie an evil. Hence the state stands in need of justification. We turn now to the project of evaluating such justifications as have been provided in the history of political philosophy.

part II

the
legitimacy
of the state

This part of this book is an argument that it is not the case that state power is legitimate. Legitimacy is defined differently in different theories of the origins and justifications of state power, and I will argue that the most familiar of these views, at any rate, fail by the standards they set themselves. I regard the assertion that the state is legitimate as equivalent to the claim that we have at least a conditional duty to obey the laws and other requirements imposed by the state, and to obey the officials of the state operating in their official capacities. Even if this duty can be overridden in certain circumstances (and every remotely plausible account of state legitimacy supposes that it can be), the state is legitimate insofar as, in the absence of overriding considerations, it imposes real duties on its citizens.

In my view the most common arguments for the legitimacy of the state in this sense fail to show that the state is legitimate on their own conceptions of legitimacy. The argument is a variety of *modus tollens*: each of these theories says that if the state is legitimate, it displays certain qualities. Because actually existing states do not display these qualities, I conclude that it's not the case that the state is legitimate. However, there could be other justifications of state power, so of course I cannot achieve the destruction of the justifications of the state once and for all, even supposing that the arguments I gave were decisive.

If there is anything that we should conclude from an examination of the traditional philosophical arguments in favor of state power, it is that they are remarkably flimsy. This I think arises especially from the fact that all of these arguments are attempts to rationalize what the thinker already believes, indeed what the thinker needs to believe most: often, for example, what butters his bread. In addition, the anarchist criticisms have long been muted or repressed, so that the arguments have often been unchallenged. Both of these weaknesses arise from the status of statism as an orthodoxy that is fundamentally accepted on faith before any argument arises: from the fact that we are born inside the state, which forms our epistemic horizon to a remarkable extent. I don't think most statist philosophers actually take seriously, deep inside, the idea that state power might be illegitimate, and hence they don't really take seriously the task of justifying it. It's very much like, say, the status of Catholic dogma in 1100 C.E.: one can hardly imagine what it would be like to think outside it, and any step outside it is impractical, extremist, or on its face ridiculous. Or it is like the five or seven or whatever arguments that Aquinas (who is also an important source of the natural law theory that underlies contractarian political philosophy) puts forward for the existence of God. They are not very good arguments, and one suspects that if comparable arguments were mounted to a different conclusion, Aquinas would recognize and expose their drawbacks. Any old argument is a good argument when it purports to establish your most cherished belief. (Of course, I'm as likely as anyone else to be subject to this particular dysfunction.)

It is worth pointing out that, just as it is impossible to detect atheist voices in the European middle ages—though I daresay every era, no matter how theocentric, generates its skeptics—it is fairly hard to find the anarchist voices in the state-ridden world; they (we) have often enough been actually repressed, but as often simply marginalized for not sharing the bedrock faith on which the world seems to stand. You can burn somebody at the stake or imprison someone, but you can also just ignore them: not publish them, dismiss them, or fail to include their position in a taxonomy of going theories, since the going theories are theories of the details of state arrangements. No one in their heart of hearts thinks state power might not be legitimate, and so everyone just kind of waves in the direction of an argument, in the touching faith that whatever colossal holes they are leaving in their theories could be patched if anyone really did doubt the assumptions on which the whole world rests. Of course anyone who raised such doubts would be an idiot, a fraud, or a monster.

chapter two

social contract

I

Those observations are aimed above all at social contract theory. I am not going to pause here to give a detailed refutation of classical contract theory, according to which a voluntary contract among future citizens is at once a serious account of the origin of the state and an account of the obligation we are under to observe the laws or decrees of the sovereign power. Almost any realistic view of the origin of states will attribute their founding, or at any rate their development and preservation, to the large-scale application of violence. The classical contract view has been destroyed so many times from so many angles that it's just kind of sad to keep piling on. One feels pity for the social contract at this point. So what I will do is give a footnote mentioning some of the outstanding refutations and make a variety of observations about a few of the classical versions, namely Hobbes, Locke, Rousseau, and about the extension of some of the basic conclusions in Hegel.[1]

Even if we do not take classical contract theory seriously on its own terms, we must accept that it has had dramatic historical effects. Locke's version has motivated the ideas of limited government, separation of powers, and respect for a written constitution (cast in contract form), and for this on a good day even an anarchist can be conditionally grateful. The idea of natural rights emerges fully only in classical social contract theory, and that view has motivated many a classical anarchist as well. However, contractarianism, like every justification of state power, also has its horrifying side. Once you claim that any given act of the state's representatives acting in their official capacity is endorsed by the "consent of the governed" (where this consent is in fact a fiction), much less by Rousseau's "general will," it is a very small step to such bizarre idols as "the dictatorship of the proletariat," wherein my arbitrary power over you, extending to every shred of your stuff and every trace of life within your organism, is justified by a confusion between my will and the "will" of a social class, or between my will and the grist mill of history, in which human beings are the grist.

A characteristic assumption or assertion of contract theory is that if the state were the result of a voluntary agreement among the people who "live under" it, the terms of that agreement could be legitimately enforced on the people who entered into it. Indeed, the assumption on most versions is that *only if* the state is a result of voluntary agreement is its authority legitimate. I agree with that entirely. It's just that there is no such agreement. Existing states did not originate in a voluntary agreement among the people who became their citizens. Even if they did so originate, that agreement could not bind the posterity of those who made it. The state does not in any sincere or serious way solicit the consent of its current citizens, and indeed it proceeds in the knowledge that if it wants, for example, to collect taxes, it had better stockpile weaponry and build prisons. As I argue below, existing states are conceptually incompatible with the very possibility of consent. Social contract theory makes what we might think of as a kind of wave in the direction of establishing the legitimacy of the state; it tries to provide the state with a mythical origin. And its apparent plausibility derives from the almost universally held basic idea that people should keep their promises.

Note that if anarchism is the view that all associations of human beings ought to be fully voluntary, then the state according to social contract theory would be compatible with anarchism. Indeed, it is worth pointing out that even large hierarchical institutions are compatible with anarchism as thus understood, as long as their power is not coercive. In fact, an examination of contract theory can help us sharpen our understanding of such notions as consent and coercion.

Classical contract theory develops in conjunction with a series of historical events: the Protestant Reformation, the civil upheavals in England in the seventeenth century, the exploration by Europeans of the terrestrial globe, and the development of the modern nation-state. If, as I urge, every account of state legitimacy can only be a response to some sort of anarchist challenge, that challenge was provided for the classical contract theorists by the most radical elements of the Reformation, the Levellers and other elements in British revolutionary politics, and, most particularly, by the ostensible "discovery" of people living without large-scale political or ecclesiastical institutions in Africa and the Americas. In such people, European intellectuals—with how much plausibility is an open question—saw their own origin. In a structure of thought from which we are not entirely released to this day, tribal peoples represented a kind of pristine or brutal state of mankind in a pre-political condition. The sting of the realization that people could exist without the hierarchical institutions of Europe was ameliorated by the idea that such people were, if people at all, savages, or people-as-animals. That view is in turn justified by the observation that these people live without a state, therefore to be an animal is to live in anarchy; to be a civilized human being is to live in thrall to state power.

This in turn coincides with the rise of modern philosophy, with its characteristic deployment of dualisms: reason and passion, man and animal, culture and nature. Among other things, this was a conception in keeping with the rise of the European state and colonialism, which matched all the pairs to the pair state and anarchy. This of course justified a policy by which indigenous peoples could be subdued and brought into some relation to coercive institutions by force of arms. But the state of nature of classical contract theory makes explicit reference to American Indians as human beings in a natural condition.

II

According to Hobbes, before the existence of the political state, people live in a "natural condition," or in the later jargon, a "state of nature."

> [I]f any two men desire the same thing, which nevertheless they cannot both enjoy, they become enemies; and in the way to their End (which is principally their owne conservation, and sometimes their delectation only) endeavour to destroy or subdue one another. . . . Hereby it is manifest that during the time men live without a common Power to keep them all in awe, they are in that condition which is called Warre; and such a warre as is of every man against every man. . . . In such condition there is no place for Industry, because the fruit thereof is uncertain: and consequently no Culture of the Earth; no navigation, nor use of the commodities that may be imported by Sea; no commodious building; no Instruments of moving and removing such things as

require much force; no Knowledge of the face of the Earth; no account of
Time; no Arts; no Letters; no Society; and which is worst of all, continual fear,
and danger of violent death; And the life of man, solitary, poor, nasty, brutish,
and short. (Hobbes, pp. 185, 186)

This is, of course, among the most famous passages in the history of political
thought, and it is worth pausing over for a moment. It expresses a dark view of
human nature, and whether or not it is accurate is a matter to which potentially all human action is relevant and to which none is. For of course human
beings as we observe them are rapacious, selfish, and brutal beyond belief, only
they are not in a state of nature. And of course people are heroic, generous,
charitable, empathetic, and so on, as well, but they are not in a state of nature.

One often feels, reading any given philosopher on the question of
"human nature," that one is reading autobiography rather than theory, or that
one is reading about the relative stability or chaos of the actual social circumstances current at a certain time and place. It is no coincidence, of course, that
the very darkest assessment of human beings, in Hobbes and Machiavelli, for
example, emerge in the midst of actual political disasters. Even more than that,
one feels that one is reading implicitly about the relation of the philosopher
to his parents, or whether he's happily married, or whether he's being sufficiently remunerated for his genius. Or perhaps one is reading a cipher of the
philosopher's serotonin levels. What I would like, I suppose, would be to read
a philosophy of "human nature" as a mixed bag, but Hobbes's basic structure
might actually be preserved under such conditions. All that is required is that
people in a state of nature are vulnerable to predation by others and that they
have a reasonable expectation of being less vulnerable once they compact to
create a sovereign power. The first of these assumptions is certainly true; the
second is certainly false.

It is remarkable that Hobbes uses the behavior of people in society as evidence of their behavior in the state of nature:

> It may seem strange to some man that has not well weighed these things that
> Nature should thus dissociate and render men apt to invade and destroy one
> another: and he may therefore, not trusting to this inference, made from the
> Passions, desire perhaps to have the same confirmed by Experience. Let him
> therefore consider with himself: when taking a journey, he armes himselfe and
> seeks to go well accompanied; when going to sleep, he locks his dores; when
> even in his house he locks his chests; and this when he knows there bee Lawes
> and publike Officers, armed, to revenge all injuries shall bee done him; what
> opinion he has of his fellow subjects, when he rides armed; of his fellow Cit-

izens, when he locks his doors; and of his children, and servants, when he
locks his chests. Does he not there as much accuse mankind by his actions as
I do by my words? (Hobbes, pp. 186–87)

This is a sort of casual remark, as if to say, let's be realistic here. The inference
goes like this: if this is the way people behave when they are subject to law
enforced by police power, imagine how much worse they would behave without it. But one might, depending on one's mood, go the other way and say: if
this is how people behave when subjected, then free them; make them responsible for themselves.

Though people were, by Hobbes's standards, living in a state of nature all
over the world when he wrote, he himself had not had the opportunity to
observe them warring each against each. It is no coincidence, as I say, that social
contract theory in its modern version coincides with the European exploration
of the globe, with European contact with people who were essentially stateless:
"For the savage people in many places of *America*, except the government of
small families, the concord whereof dependeth on natural lust, have no government at all, and live at this day in that brutish manner" (Hobbes, p. 187). The
idea of a social contract as the origin of the political state is ancient. What is
new in Hobbes is precisely the idea of a state of nature, or at least its elaborate
exploration. This is itself a political move, or it responds to the nascent anarchist
challenge—fully realized in romanticism—of people living without a state in
any European sense. Hobbes's state of nature is a defense of European culture
against an imagined critique by the savages of America. It is important, of
course, to realize that Hobbes had no first-hand knowledge of the lives of such
savages, and so he describes them with reference to the behavior of the savages
of the British middle classes.

Indeed, if it turns out that there has been no real contract in the Hobbesian sense, then it turns out that the British middle classes are by Hobbes's standard still in a state of nature, which is certainly compatible with their being
governed by a state that rests on force. Then the state becomes simply part of
the chaotic violence of the state of nature. One might speculate, once one
accepts that the natural state is as Hobbes suggests, that people in that state
might not merely make war each on each, but might band together in temporary groups to rape, kill, and rob more successfully, a merely prudential development and an obvious one. This would leave us in the moral vacuum of the
state of nature while also creating various nodes and centers of power. That is
precisely the case.

In Robert Nozick's state of nature, people slowly contract for mutual protection against predators; they hire a protective association that eventually must

monopolize deadly force in a given area and become a state. We might think about the choice of people in the state of nature more proactively. It's not that they're only figuring out how to protect themselves; it's that they're working rationally on the problem of how to achieve maximum rapine and sack. Now it will quickly become obvious that you face two possible roles: pillager or victim. Anyone with any tendency toward rational choice theory can see the answer. You should not be surprised if the pillagers realize that membership in the pillagers is worth something, so you'll be paying a tribute from now on because you're under our protection. Putting it gently, that is no less plausible than the Hobbes/Nozick scenario, but then one could hardly hold that the legitimacy of this state rests on a contract when the situation is entirely coerced.

There is one remarkable feature of state of nature theory in its classical forms. The moment of social contract is the moment wherein nature is transcended, the moment when animal becomes spirit. The savage is precisely the human being as animal body; the civilized, state-subordinated man is the human being as spirit. We can literally transcend by means of the social contract the filthy plain of the merely physical and animal. This is one of many reasons why social contract theory, despite all appearances of good sense and rationality, is in its essence a religious orientation: it promises an apotheosis. And when it reaches its full flower, wherein even the contract is left behind, when we fly through Rousseau to Hegel, the state is our becoming-identical to God.

Hobbes continues:

> To this war of every man against every man, this also is consequent; that nothing can be Unjust. The notions of Right and Wrong, Justice and Injustice, have there no place. Where there is no common Power, there is no Law; where no Law, no Injustice. . . . Justice and Injustice are none of the Faculties neither of the Body nor Mind. If they were, they might be in a man that were alone in the world, as well as his Senses and Passions. They are Qualities, that relate to men in Society, not in Solitude. (Hobbes, p. 188)

For Hobbes, as for many philosophers of many kinds in the Western tradition, mere nature can have no moral content; *is* never entails *ought*, for example; values are not among the descriptive inventory of facts about the world as a physical system, including descriptions of animals such as Homo sapiens. This means that the moment of contract is an extraordinary moment, the human moment, the moment at which values come to be, at which we cease to be natural creatures and become rational creatures: "where no Covenant hath preceded, there hath no Right been transferred, and every man has a right to every thing; and consequently, no action can be Unjust. But when a Covenant is made, then to break it is *Unjust*: and the definition of INJUSTICE, is no other than *the not Performance of Covenant*. And whatsoever is not Unjust, is *Just*" (Hobbes, p. 202). What we have in the state of nature are certain powers, the exercise of which has no moral content. Our emergence into government is emergence into a moral world.

Here is Hobbes's famous description of the moment of our caterpillar/butterfly metamorphosis from animal to spirit:

> The only way to erect such a Common Power, as may be able to defend them from the invasion of Foreigners, and the injuries of one another, and thereby to secure them in such sort, as that by their owne industrie and by the fruites of the Earth they may nourish themselves and live contentedly, is to conferre all their power and strength upon one Man, or upon one Assembly of men, that may reduce all their Wills, by plurality of voices, unto one Will: which is as much as to say, to appoint one man, or Assembly of men, to beare their Person; and every one to owne and acknowledge himselfe to be Author of whatsoever he that so beareth their Person, shall Act, or cause to be Acted, in those things which concern the Common Peace and Safetie; and therein to submit their Wills, every one to his Will, and their Judgements to his Judgement. This is more than Consent, or Concord; it is a reall Unitie of them all, in one and the same Person, made by Covenant of every man with every man, in such manner as if every man should say to every man: *I Authorise and give up my Right of Governing my selfe, to this Man, or to this Assembly of men, on this condition; that thou give up, thy Right to him, and Authorise all his Actions in like manner.* This done, the Multitude so united in one person is called a COMMONWEALTH; in Latin, CIVITAS. This is the generation of that great LEVIATHAN, or rather (to speake more reverently) of that *Mortall God* to which wee owe, under the *Immortal God*, our peace and defence. (Hobbes, p. 227)

In the previous few chapters, Hobbes has been investigating the notion of contract under British common law in a stolid commonsense sort of fashion. But here his language rises in rhapsody. The creation of a sovereign power joins distinct animal bodies together into a single will; it makes the group a unity in the same sense that a single person is a unity. Hobbesian rhapsody is the tone of the modern era in political philosophy, which is the poetry of state power, a kind of ecstatic masochistic affirmation of human subjection as the very origin of humanity itself. It is an apotheosis of the self and its erasure into a social nirvana, the joining of our wills together in the ocean of general will, our becoming-identical with God, or possibly Warren G. Harding.

And this unity of us all, by which we transcend animality and individuality, this mortal God, etc., to whom we owe our very lives puts us in infinite debt.

[B]ecause every Subject is by this Institution Author of all the Actions and Judgements of the Soveraigne Instituted; it followes that whatsoever he doth, can be no injury to any of his Subjects; nor ought he to be by any of them accused of Injustice. For he that doth anything by authority from another, doth therein no injury to him by whose authority he acteth: But by this Institution of a Common-wealth every particular man is Author of all the Soveraigne doth; and consequently he that complaineth of injury from his Soveraigne complaineth of that whereof he himself is Author, and therefore ought not to accuse any man but himselfe; no, nor himselfe of injury, because to do injury to ones selfe is impossible. (Hobbes, p. 232)

Here we have as monstrous and absurd a political doctrine as has ever been enunciated, but it follows (though perhaps with some qualifications) on any view wherein wills are united in fiction while remaining distinct in fact, on the views of Rousseau, Hegel, and Marx, for instance. When the Khmer Rouge starts stacking skulls, they do so by the will of the people whose skulls they stack.

One of the many fearsome aspects of this philosophy is that in the delusion that we have emerged from a world of violence and chaos, it authorizes violence and chaos. Even if it did not explicitly grant the sovereign the power to rape, pillage, and kill, which it explicitly does, it is a massive self-delusion that justifies genocide. When we come across the savages of America, on this view, or anyone in a stateless condition, we are human beings coming across animals, spirits flitting among the pigs and dogs. There is no justice among the savages of America, and no injustice can be inflicted on them. Thus we refute the idea of anarchism by a series of arguments identical to mass graves.

III

Locke's version of social contract, though structurally identical (state of nature—contract—sovereign political state), is, of course, an argument for democracy rather than arbitrary monarchy. Although it is perhaps not a purely philosophical observation, I might remark that it is preferable if measured by its intended results. It also has an important moment of direct argumentative superiority over Hobbes's version: the idea that people in a state of nature, as they form a compact, would place themselves under the arbitrary and unlimited power of a sovereign is incompatible with the reasons for which they enter the compact in the first place.

Obviously, Locke has a sunnier outlook on mankind in a state of nature:

> To understand political power aright, and derive it from its original, we must consider what estate all men are naturally in, and that is, a state of perfect freedom to order their actions, and dispose of their possessions and persons as they think fit, within the bounds of the law of Nature, without asking leave or depending upon the will of any other man.
>
> A state also of equality, wherein all the power and jurisdiction is reciprocal, no one having more than another, there being nothing more evident than that creatures of the same species and rank, promiscuously born to all the same advantages of Nature, and the use of the same faculties, should also be equal one amongst another, without subordination or subjection, unless the lord and master of them all should, by any manifest declaration of his will, set one above another, and confer on him, by an evident and clear appointment, an undoubted right to dominion and sovereignty.[2]

Unlike Hobbes's state of nature, Locke's has moral content. In fact, by a coincidence that must have pleased Locke, the moral laws of a state of nature are precisely the principles of classical liberalism:

> The state of Nature has a law of Nature to govern it, which obliges every one, and reason, which is that law, teaches all mankind who will but consult it, that being all equal and independent, no one ought to harm another in his life, health, liberty or possessions; for men being all the workmanship of one omnipotent and infinitely wise Maker; all the servants of one sovereign Master, sent into the world by His order and about His business; they are His property, whose workmanship they are made to last during His, not one another's pleasure. And, being furnished with like faculties, sharing all in one community of Nature, there cannot be supposed any such subordination among us that may authorise us to destroy one another, as if we were made for one another's uses, as the inferior ranks of creatures are for ours. Every one as he is bound to preserve himself, and not to quit his station wilfully, so by the like reason, when his own preservation comes not in competition, ought he as much as he can to preserve the rest of mankind, and not unless it be to do justice on an offender, take away or impair the life, or what tends to the preservation of the life, the liberty, health, limb, or goods of another. (Locke, pp. 5, 6)

The theological tone here (and Locke's appeal at this moment to Hooker's *Ecclesiastical Politie*, an explicitly theocentric contract theory) must be taken seriously, though Locke has received an ever more secular reception. His law of nature is Aquinas's; it is the eternal law of God, insofar as it is given to human reason to be able to understand it, in application to the moral conduct of human life. It is important to see that there is essentially no secular or philosophical justification for this view in Locke, though he appeals to the self-evidence of the analogy of each of us to each of us.

The natural law yields natural rights, and though Hobbes occasionally hints at such an idea, he did not think people had any natural rights in the way that Locke or Jefferson conceived natural rights: as a zone of autonomy around the life, liberty, and property of each person that others are bound to observe. Unless natural rights follow directly from the laws of God—and even if they do, since there is no argument that they do—I think there is essentially no argument in Locke for natural rights except a kind of appeal to each person's sense of themselves. But for me, I must say, that appeal is enough, and whether or not a rational defense or even a clear conception of natural or (as I would prefer to phrase it) inherent rights is really possible, I myself believe, deep down, that I possess such rights. Thus I think the form of argument in Locke, a kind of appeal to self-evidence and intuition, is the right form of argument, or at least sufficient to suggest that if each person is sincere and consistent, they will believe themselves to have inherent rights and will attribute them to others. The argument, that is, can be made to rest on theological faith, or it can be made to rest on secular faith rooted in self-reflection. Locke tries to do both; I myself can only endorse the latter.

If someone takes something that I regard as mine, I feel violated. If someone will not let me speak in a matter that concerns me, I don't interpret this merely as a clash of force; I believe that I have a right to express myself. In short, there is a zone of autonomy surrounding my action that I must believe has some moral force and makes some moral claim on other people. This belief of mine may be no more than my acculturation, especially since I live in a polity that is built on a Lockean foundation, and especially since I am sympathetic to any view that conduces to human freedom. But why am I sympathetic to any argument that conduces to human freedom? Fundamentally because I feel myself inherently to be free. Indeed, this even extends to the idea that people are equal in the Declaration-of-Independence-type sense: I feel that you, no matter what your office may be, have no more right to tell me how to live than I have to tell you how to live.

I'm enough of a positivist to believe that basic moral and political views are fundamentally emotional commitments. I will not rest arguments in favor of anarchism on natural rights, unless I signal explicitly that I am foregoing any pretension to establish them on a rational basis. However, I can do what Locke implicitly does: I can ask you to what extent you value your autonomy and how you think about that autonomy. But to understand Locke, you must see that his axiology has a completely different foundation than Hobbes's. For Hobbes, there is no justice outside covenant; justice is merely observance of covenant. That is why the emergence from the state of nature is an ontological epiphany, turning us from animals to souls. This is not true of Locke, and that is the most profound difference between Locke and Hobbes: as it applies to people, nature itself, for Locke, possesses moral content; even in the state of nature, we are not mere animals.

At any rate, the autonomy delineated by the laws of God and the natural rights of man are vulnerable in a state of nature. In particular, property is vulnerable to the incursions of those irrational or desperate enough not to understand the natural state of justice. The fact that Locke rests the necessity of the state largely on the preservation of property rights (which would entail, among other things, that the contractors would not want to constitute a sovereign with an unlimited power to tax) has often enough been used to accuse Locke of being to bourgeois ideology what Marx is to proletarian ideology. For present purposes, however, that is neither here nor there.

If one believes in natural rights, it is evident that state power often violates them, though it may also in other circumstances preserve them. Locke draws the conclusion from this that the power of the individual can only be given over to the state in a voluntary act. It would follow that only on a contractual basis can state power be legitimately constituted:

> Men being, as has been said, by nature, all free, equal, and independent, no one can be put out of this estate, and subjected to the political power of another, without his own consent. The only way whereby any one divests himself of his natural liberty, and puts on the bonds of civil society, is by agreeing with other men to join and unite into a community for their comfortable, safe, and peaceable living one amongst another, in a secure enjoyment of their properties, and a greater security against any, that are not of it. This any number of men may do, because it injures not the freedom of the rest; they are left as they were in the liberty of the state of nature. When any number of men have so consented to make one community or government, they are thereby presently incorporated, and make one body politic, wherein the majority have a right to act and conclude the rest. (Locke, p. 54)

The "body politic" idea is a mild version of Hobbes's Leviathan, but Locke is strangely enthusiastic about collective consciousness and social bodies consisting of many scattered human bodies: "it is in their legislative, that the members of a commonwealth are united, and combined together into one coherent living body. This is the soul that gives form, life, and unity, to the commonwealth" (p. 120). The legislative appears in this function because, aside from his positions with regard to Parliament and the crown, or maybe not aside from this, Locke holds the legislative function to be the site of sovereignty as the source of law, the source of political obligation. I call this enthusiasm strange because Locke is often accused of rampant individualism, of regarding each person as an atom. This accusation is just in the sense that individuals are more or less atomic in the state of nature, but Locke also yearns toward the collective identity or consciousness that a contract supposedly makes possible.

No less than Hobbes, of course, Locke needs a notion of tacit consent, since it is just not true that most of us consent explicitly, reflectively, and so on. If the notion of tacit consent cannot be clarified in a fashion from which it plausibly follows that the average person living in the average polity has consented, then by Locke's standards we are under no obligation to obey the state. For Locke, only consent can give legitimacy to state power, but under most conditions consent is not explicit, so the legitimacy of the state depends upon paying off on the notion of tacit consent. The arguments concerning tacit consent are among the most exhausted in philosophy. I would prefer just to take it as read that the arguments are bad, but I am going to have to have some engagement.

Let me note, to begin with, that consent is always compromised by force; the mere existence of effective force dedicated to some end constitutes coercion toward that end, whatever you may think or want. If I consent to abide by the law when that law is enforced by a huge body of men with guns and clubs, it is never clear, to say the least, whether my consent is genuine or not. The mere possession of overwhelming force entails that my consent is not required in order for the state to alienate my rights in any particular way. It will always be prudent for me, under such circumstances, to simulate consent, and there are no clear signs by which a simulation could be distinguished from a genuine consent in such a case. That I am enthusiastic in my acquiescence to your overwhelming capacity for violence—that I pledge my allegiance according to formula, sing patriotic songs and so on—does not entail that I am not merely acquiescing. The claim, common to all states and criterial for them in the anarchist view, to a monopoly of coercion resting on deadly force is incompatible with the claim that participation is voluntary. The police power of the state in its actual operation puts the lie to the claim that the state is based practically on the consent of the governed. The ambition of the state to an overwhelming and exclusive use of force makes consent, even if it could exist, irrelevant.

The idea that any state is a voluntary association of human beings can be refuted by looking at actual cases of voluntary association of human beings.

Paradigms would be clubs, PTAs, bake sale committees, and the like. If the administrators of the local high school strutted around your neighborhood with grenades hanging on their belts, then suggested that you might want to join the PTA, it would hardly be possible to say whether anyone's participation was voluntary or not. That is, the mere existence of an overwhelming force by which the laws will be enforced compromises conceptually the possibility of voluntarily acceding to them. Or put it this way: the power of the government, constituted by hypothesis under contract, by which it preserves the liberties and properties of its citizens, is itself conceptually incompatible with the very possibility of their consent.

Consent is not an intrinsic state of an individual person; it is a feature of a person in a setting. The choice must be objectively free or the consent is compromised. In a situation where I push you off a cliff, whether you consented to fall is neither here nor there; in a situation like that, consent is conceptually precluded, even if you intended to jump. In a situation where you knew that if you did not jump, I would push you, and that resistance and evasion were practically impossible (say because I have brought a heavily-armed force), you cannot jump voluntarily. Voluntary action, in a political context, is conceptually incompatible with overwhelming coercive force. One problem is that the actual mechanisms by which consent is supposedly expressed—tacit contracts and so on—are radically inadequate. But the situation is much worse than that. It's not only that I do not (or do) consent, but that it is impossible for me either to consent or not to consent; the objective situation compromises the very possibility of voluntary action. Obviously the state is not all that interested, really, in your consent, but it makes voluntary action impossible in relation to its decisions and institutions by overwhelmingly constraining your choice situation.

In a situation in which my decision is hedged around with penalties, the distinction between acquiescence and consent loses all purchase. This is as true, or truer, in cases of "tacit consent" as or than in cases of explicit acquiescence. When, say, failing to uproot my life and family and enter a different culture (and for that matter, one in which I face all the same sort of constraints) is taken as evidence of my consent, a kind of category mistake has been made; in a case like that, consent is not in question at all. When it is a matter of accepting benefits which I cannot choose to forego, paying for these benefits in a manner I cannot avoid (as in income or sales taxes), it is not merely laughable and disingenuous to say I have consented, it is just a conceptual error, like saying something tastes pink.

It is, again, not only a sheer matter of being forced; it is a matter of being in a situation in which the range of choice is in fact constrained. Of course the state never rests its legitimacy day by day on your consent, never seeks your tax dollars as a charitable contribution, but finds a thousand ways to make sure that you acquiesce. A situation in which you can either acquiesce or by heroic measures resist is a situation in which consent is not in question. It's not a matter of possibly ceasing to consent; your consent was never in play at all. Social contract theory is, hence, conceptually incoherent at its heart, not only false but senseless, the merest paradox.

This issue is similar in some ways to the question of whether and in what sense human action is free or voluntary in a world in which each event is fully determined by previous events, given the laws of physics. This is one of the most bewildering thickets in philosophy, where it is called "the free will problem." And we must throw in the further question of whether, in a deterministic universe, or with only whatever freedom one may have in such a universe, one is morally responsible for one's actions. Consider an analogue in the political case. Each morning, the state issues a detailed schedule of my day. Furthermore, I have been assigned a personal coercer. He follows me around and has an elaborate list of the actions I am supposed to take in the course of a given day: turn left at this corner; pee at 5:10; watch General Hospital, and so on. If I deviate from this schedule even slightly, my personal coercer is to shoot me; I am not in a position to resist or shoot back. Now as it happens, by a massive coincidence, the state's schedule coincides precisely with what I want to do with my day, or at least just what I would have done anyway. And so I escape death, not primarily or at least not only because I do what I'm told, but because I do what I want. Now the question is: do I act freely?

It's a wicked question, and a ridiculous case, but it is not entirely irrelevant. Probably most people obey the laws, file their tax returns more or less on time and more or less accurately, and so on. Most people do not come face to face with coercion every day, though many people, such as prisoners, do. This is, again, highly analogous to the free will/determinism issue, with the coercer playing the universe and the laws of physics, but the political case must be adjudicated on completely different, let's say psychological, grounds. First of all, in the imagined case, you would certainly (I hope) resent the presence of the coercer and experience that presence as a limitation on your political freedom. Yes? You might even be tempted to act in ways you would not have acted otherwise to see whether you actually had any scope for initiative or independence. Indeed, it might become impossible for you to know how you would have acted if there were no coercer. If you became accustomed to the presence of the coercer and his schedule, you would quickly take to a routinized existence; you would, after a period of training or a continuous routine, cease to be fully aware of the coercion lurking beneath your everyday actions. It would not follow, I think, that as your awareness lapsed, your freedom grew. Quite the reverse.

This little thought experiment is similar to one famously presented by Harry Frankfurt. Frankfurt argues that you are morally responsible for your actions in certain sorts of cases where you could not have done otherwise: namely where you are constrained to do what you would have done anyway.[3] Here we consider the example from a political perspective rather than first as bearing on individual responsibility. In the society we are imagining and in the society in which we live, the question of what you would have done if you were not hedged around by restrictions is impossible to answer, given that the shape of your world is massively articulated by the institutions of the state and by other persons, whose lives are also so shaped. The truth conditions on the counterfactual are merely chaotic. In such a situation, determining whether you could or could not have done otherwise is precisely that hard or fantastic; you are imagining your way back through generations to a pristine world. Assigning moral responsibility in anyone's sense—compatibilist or incompatibilist, determinist or believer in freedom—is equally problematic, for whether you would have done the same without the external constraints is as impossible to fix plausibly, or is a question just as fraught, as whether you could have done otherwise.

In any case, consider a point of view external to the society of perfect compatibilism we are imagining. Where every person is followed around by an agent of the state with a piece of paper and a loaded pistol, anyone in their right mind would call such a state totalitarian, and would understand that, if the insane massive coincidence of desire and external power broke down, the bloodbath would ensue. I don't think anyone would simply eyeball this as a free society. If that is right, then political coercion is not a matter simply of not being able to do what you want, but of being in a situation in which other people are articulating your choices by force. If that is the case, then situations in which anyone can be expunged by the state at any time, as is true more or less of all individuals in modernity, the state does not rest on consent. Let me repeat my result: the very existence of the state in its manifestation of overwhelming irresistible force is incompatible with the very possibility of consent. We might put the irony at the heart of contract theory like this: the conditions of state power constituted legitimately under contract are entirely incompatible with the idea that people can consent or that the state rests on the consent of the governed. Celebrating the result of consent with coercion, lionizing consent as the only source of legitimate power, contract theorists erase it conceptually.

The problem extends to the moral implications of determinism. In a world where political freedom is radically curtailed by coercion to the point at which consent is neither needed nor possible, people's actions cease to have moral content. It may be that moral responsibility is compatible with determinism; it may even be that if a chain of causation proceeds through your body, though you could not have done otherwise, you are responsible for the outcomes of the event under certain circumstances. But where the event proceeds from the decision of another who applies force to make your body comply, there the decision and the responsibility lies fundamentally with the coercer. Coercing people reduces the moral content of their lives, reduces them to the status of inanimate objects. To seek systematically to reduce the scope of freedom, however freedom is understood metaphysically, is to attack the status of human beings as moral agents.

Many anarchists have equated state power with slavery. State power and slavery certainly have this in common: they tear down the status of a human being as a moral agent or center of action. This is destructive enough, but when it is simultaneously asserted that the purpose of state power is human freedom, the result ought to be nausea. If one is going to endorse universal coercion, one should do so frankly and with a good conscience. The state really does seek universal coercion in that it hedges each person round with a coercive structure that is globally incompatible with moral agency. This is, I believe, one of the reasons people actually express loyalty to the state: they want to offload the burden of their own agency. In any case, such a strategy comports extremely poorly with a picture of the human being as the possessor of natural rights or as a free party to a contract. Even philosophers who are enthusiastic about contractarianism—Rawls and Nozick have this, if nothing else, in common, for example—have withdrawn the claim that the authority of democratic polities rests on the consent of the governed, and have rendered social contract theory over into a mere conceptual exercise. This takes their justifications into a different category, as I shall discuss later.

At any rate, anyone who holds that legitimate state power can only rest on the consent of the governed is an anarchist. Here is a forthright statement of anarchist political philosophy: "Men being, as has been said, by nature all free, equal, and independent, no one can be put out of this estate and subjected to the political power of another without his own consent." It's a lovely ideal, the anarchist ideal; it's just that it's not actualized. The condition on which alone social contract theory recognizes a state as legitimate is that the state is an anarchy.

One note before we leave Locke: the fact that he, in comparison with Hobbes, moves from a more positive assessment of human nature to the design of a government that displays limited powers and preserves more than a semblance of freedom has helped to prop up the common sense that these things vary in correlation. The better people are, the more they can be trusted to govern themselves, the more freedom they can retain against state coercion. This is a non sequitur, given that the people being entrusted with power have on the whole the same goodness or badness as the people over whom their power is exercised, given that these people, too, are people. We will explore this theme in the discussion of utilitarianism.

IV

I have found myself giving at least cursory arguments against Hobbes and Locke, though it is the diagnosis, not the refutation, that I would like to emphasize. When I turn now to Rousseau and Hegel, I will forego refutation entirely, resting content primarily with ridicule. This is partly a matter of the characteristics of their authorship. Rousseau's account of the social contract and state legitimacy is riddled with ambivalences or outright contradictions overlain with a layer of obscurities. Hegel has a way of absorbing refutations like a sort of goo; any objection one might make will just be caught up in the process from which the structure of thought is already emerging. And really, there are no arguments in Hegel or Rousseau anyway. Hegel, as is well known, explicitly rejected the contract theory, and Rousseau's account is thin: there is little weight on the contract itself, except as a sign of an emerging general will. Nevertheless, Rousseau resorts to classical contract theory, and Hegel follows hard on Rousseau.

I read both Rousseau and Hegel as outright totalitarians, and I will try to say why. It's not that they regarded themselves as totalitarians; quite the reverse. However, it is worth pointing out that most totalitarians, and certainly including the most vicious, do not consider themselves totalitarians. And it's not that Rousseau and Hegel didn't pay tribute elaborately to human freedom both metaphysically and in the context of state power. It's just that what they actually prescribe practically entails a totalitarian state. One might also mention that their notions of freedom are, shall we say, disturbing.

The idea that the political state is a single "body" which, as Aristotle famously put it, is "prior" to the individual,[4] has been called the "organic" conception of the state. It is usually opposed to individualist conceptions captured in classical contract theory, in which the state is the result of the rational, self-interested decisions of discrete persons. Here is Rousseau's statement, a commonplace by the time he writes: "Immediately, in place of the individual person of each contracting party, this act of association creates an artificial and collective body, composed of as many members as there are voters in the assembly and by this same act [which entails "the total alienation by each associate of himself and all his rights"] that body acquires its unity, its common *ego*, its life and will."[5] In both Hobbes and Locke, particularly Hobbes, the individualist and organic conceptions are both present, and the attempt is made to show the generation of the state organism, or Leviathan, out of the individuals who compose it. In Hegel, the organic conception reaches its culmination: "If the 'people' is represented . . . as an inwardly developed, genuinely organic, totality, then sovereignty is there as the personality of the whole."[6] One could hardly be an anarchist if one didn't have an instinctual revulsion for organic conceptions of the state, which we see in contemporary thought most clearly in the movement known as "communitarianism."

Be that as it may, it is certain that, whatever the totalitarian implications, Rousseau took himself to be articulating a vision of human liberation and to entirely reject power that rested merely on force. "Force is a physical power; I do not see how its effects could produce morality. To yield to force is an act of necessity, not of will; it is at best an act of prudence. In what sense can it be a moral duty?" (Rousseau, p. 52). But then his own account of sovereignty appears to authorize unlimited use of force precisely by defining force away in an a priori fashion as a feature of sovereignty. That is, sovereignty cannot be a matter of force. Therefore, when the sovereign power arrests you, beats you down, and executes you, it is not in fact using force at all:

> Now, as the sovereign is formed entirely of the individuals who compose it, it has not, nor could it ever have any interest contrary to theirs; and so the sovereign power has no need to give guarantees to its subjects, because it is impossible for the body to wish to hurt all its members, and, as we shall see, it cannot hurt any particular member. The sovereign, by the mere fact that it is, is always all that it ought to be. (Rousseau, p. 63)

Or we have this:

> [I]n order then that the social pact shall not be an empty formula, it is tacitly implied in that commitment—which alone can give force to all others—that whoever refuses to obey the general will shall be constrained to do so by the whole body, which means nothing less than that he shall be forced to be free; for this is the condition which, by giving each citizen to the nation, secures him against all personal dependence, it is the condition which shapes both the design and the working of the political machine, and which alone bestows justice on civil contracts—without it, such contracts would be absurd, tyrannical and liable to the grossest abuses. (Rousseau, p. 64)

We have traversed a similar set of assertions in Hobbes, though he has better sense than to resort to such formulations as the repulsive "forced to be free."

And in Hobbes of course there is no doubt about the totalitarian tendencies, which—and this is one of the refreshing aspects of Hobbes—are clearly stated and frankly avowed. As I say, however, Rousseau takes himself to be articulating a vision of liberation. The only interpretation I could give to this beyond sheer insincerity or sheer self-deception would be that, insofar as one's individual will participates in the making of the sovereign power, one really does—literally, on reflection, at the moment of truth—affirm the authority that punishes or constrains one.

The question of Rousseau's totalitarianism, of course, turns on the pivotal and elusive conception of a "general will." Let me allow that the faculty of decision or will is not always confined to an individual human organism and, in fact, always engages or encompasses an external world. In communication with other persons, it is possible to reach decisions together that all the parties can endorse as their own decisions. And it is possible to be swept away by the decision of a multitude, to lose one's will into a crowd, as it were. There are many actual social mechanisms of many kinds for collective deliberation. So I do not want to make a simple presumption of individualism; I do not want to assert simply that the only thing moved by a singular will is a singular body. It is not at all clear what procedures Rousseau would suggest for the construction of a general will or for political deliberation, but if this sort of mundane collective decision-making is what Rousseau means by a general will, then by all means.

But I will insist upon this much, and I ask you whether you do not agree with me: the individual is also a locus of will, and it is always possible, with regard to any subject-matter in any situation, for one person's will to be pitted against another or against many others. In whatever manner a given interpersonal will may be constructed, no matter the number or identity of the people who compose it or the procedures by which they deliberate, it is possible for any individual human will to oppose it. It is possible to disagree with a consensus, to refuse to take part in a collective deliberative activity, or to disavow its results. This is true with regard to every single act of collective decision. It may be that a collective decision of many people should overrule the will of a single dissenter. It may be that the dissenter should be punished or constrained for his dissent or for the actions he takes contrary to the collective decision. It may be that the consensus from which the dissenter demurs represents the best our species can be at a given moment, or the essential spirit of the culture from which it emerges, or the command of a benevolent God. Still it is possible to dissent.

Much ink has been spilled trying to assign a meaning to Rousseau's "general will," a project toward which I am sufficiently hostile to regard as silly. At any rate, the idea would be to remove to the comforting world of counterfactuals: the general will is what we would all will if we were all rational; if we were all aware of own real interests; if the political system were perfectly responsive to the majority, or something. I am happy to play with each of those baubles, but let me say this: either it is possible for the individual will to contradict the general will, or it is not. If you say that it is not, I accuse you of the merest fascism, but I also still don't know what you mean. For obviously it is possible for the individual will right now to contradict the will we would share if we were all rational, or if we were aware of our real interests, or if we lived in a perfect democracy. And if the individual will can, after all, contradict the general will, then many passages in *The Social Contract* are merely incomprehensible. Indeed it can, and indeed they are.

What Rousseau actually means by the general will, since he evidently believes that it is impossible to demur from it, grows ever more obscure with each assertion about it he makes. But he cannot mean (can he?) that dissent from some consensus is by definition impossible. I say that we all know this by experience. I say that we all know this by the most cursory examination of history. And I say we ought to believe this because the alternative is a view that will (and has) been used to justify massive repressions, purges, genocides. I would advise this: do not let any particular jargon or sump of ideology drive you to the point at which you hold not that those who disagree with you are wrong, but that they do not and cannot actually disagree with you. That is the moment of megalomania in Rousseau and in the lives of actual dictatorships. Of course, if I say that it is false, that is, I suppose, to delude myself into thinking that I could reject the onward flow of history, or whatever.

In Rousseau we experience the emergence of the totalitarian left, the obscure premonition of Mao and Stalin, whose status as embodiments of general will forced millions to be free of the shackles of life itself.

V

In *Philosophy of Right*, Hegel praises Rousseau for resting his account of the state on general will, but he attacks Rousseau for resorting to a contract, with its implied individualism. The picture of individual free agents contracting to form a state is incompatible with the organic status that Hegel ascribes to it, and it is incompatible with "the absolutely divine principle of the state, together with its majesty and authority" (*Philosophy of Right*, p. 153). No polity is constituted in the contractarian sense, and there is no moment of origin at which the state emerges from individuals: "It is absolutely essential that the constitution should not be regarded as something made, even though it has come to being in time. It must be treated rather as something simply existent in and by itself, as divine therefore, and constant, and so exalted above the sphere of things that are made" (*Philosophy of Right*, p. 178).

Hegel's political philosophy, notoriously, has been used to justify almost everything: communism, fascism, liberal democracy. But for all the obscurities of his prose, one thing is certain about Hegel: no one has ever waxed so rhapsodic about the state; no one has loved the very idea of the state as Hegel did. And no one has ever inflated its dignity and grandeur with such maniac earnestness. The state for Hegel is love and truth and freedom and beauty and reason and, in short, God: "The state is the divine will, in the sense that it is mind present on earth, unfolding itself to be the actual shape and organization of the world" (*Philosophy of Right*, p. 166). Of course Hegel is abstracting from the concrete accidents of any given actual state, which are riddled with petty corruptions and colossal incompetences, power-hungry thugs and impossible bureaucracies. We must not, Hegel says, take "external appearances" as the state's "substance," for that would ignore the state's "absolute infinity." Tell you what. Though it cost me my self-respect, I will submit unconditionally to Mind, on the condition of my complete release from Mindlessness. I will submit unconditionally to absolute infinity, on the condition of my complete release from all purported obligations imposed by the state's mere external appearance.

Many, notably Shlomo Avineri and Charles Taylor, have tried to defend Hegel from the charge of state-worship, which is pitiful and is an index only of their own state-worship, or more probably their Hegel-worship. It's not that there aren't interesting and influential moments in Hegel's political philosophy, but whatever is worth recovering must also have something to do with what Hegel actually said. Indeed, no sooner has Taylor called the charge of state worship "wide of the mark" than he quotes the *Lectures on Philosophy of History*: "Everything that man is he owes to the state; only in it can he find his essence. All value that a man has, all spiritual reality, he has only through the state."[7] It would be interesting to know what Taylor might actually count as "state-worship"—perhaps cleaning the shoes of the police force each morning with one's tongue.

Hegel deploys a particularly intense and serious version of a view we have already seen in classical contract theory: that the state is opposed to mere nature, and human beings are raised by and in the state to mind, civilization, history. Rousseau's is a typical description of the ontological transformation from body to spirit accomplished by submission:

> The passing from the state of nature to the civil society produces a remarkable change in man; it puts justice as a rule of conduct in place of instinct, and gives his actions the moral quality they previously lacked. It is only then, when

the voice of duty has taken the place of physical impulse, and right that of desire, that man, who has hitherto thought only of himself, finds himself compelled to act on other principles, and to consult his reason rather than study his inclinations. And although in civil society man surrenders some of the advantages that belong to the state of nature, he gains in return far greater ones; his faculties are so exercised and developed, his mind is so enlarged, his sentiments so ennobled, and his whole spirit so elevated that, if the abuse of his new condition did not in many cases lower him to something worse than what he had left, he should constantly bless the happy hour that lifted him for ever from the state of nature, and, from a narrow, stupid animal, made him a creature of intelligence and a man. (Rousseau, 64–5)

The moment of emergence into a state is the moment of transcendence of the physical plane. The relation of the state to nature is dualism writ large: it is the relation of mind to body bloated up into the whole species. And though people may continue to act like animals, and for that matter may still be hairy and give birth to live young in the manner of mammals and so on, they have the bureaucracy to thank for their surprising ability to float free of the degradation of embodiment. The state is our salvation. Many of its actions may appear to be the work of animals—greedy, passion-ridden apes. But that is a mere accident. Behind them lurks Mind Itself, luring us all to a transcendence of the physical, by the immolation of millions of live human bodies, if necessary. "As high as mind stands above nature, so high does the state stand above life. Man must therefore venerate the state as a secular deity, and observe that if it is difficult to comprehend nature, it is infinitely harder to comprehend the state" (*Philosophy of Right*, 285). Here I would certainly agree. All of the pathetic attempts of empirical science to understand the world, up to the outer reaches of cosmology or quantum mechanics or string theory, are child's play in comparison to the attempt to penetrate the infinite yapping of bureaucrats, to say nothing of the Groveling Humbuggery of Hegel's political philosophy.

V

The historical origin of the state is not consent, but submission. And the function of contract theory is simply this: to call submission consent or transcendence, fantastically to preserve one's pride in the face of one's degradation. The history we have just traversed is a masochist ecstasy.

chapter three

utilitarian justifications of
state power

I

Hobbes rests the legitimacy of state power on compact. But he rests the compact on utility; what motivates the contractors is the misery of life with no sovereign power. Whenever I delicately mention my sympathy with an anarchist position, the first response I get is that state power is absolutely essential to prevent what my interlocutors loosely represent along the lines of a Hobbesian war of every man against every man. People are self-interested, brutal, short-sighted, dishonest; they will attempt to get away with anything they can, and they must be restrained by rules and rulers. Anarchism would be a good political philosophy for angels, but people are closer to demons. Well, perhaps not, but some people are demonic, and they must be restrained. Law is the only thing between us and chaos, between decent people and whomever is strongest, most brutal, most bereft of conscience, or most heavily armed. Anarchy is massively impractical; state power is a necessity.

One thing I notice about this argument: it is almost always self-congratu-latory. Very few people believe of themselves that the only thing that keeps them from raping and pillaging is a police force. But they always believe it of someone; they are perhaps picturing poor folks or black folks, people without the sturdy good sense and good intentions of people like us. And I would sug-gest not that all this is necessarily false in any particular case, but that if you think that you yourself could behave decently in the absence of men with guns telling you what to do, or bookshelf-length lists of statutes and so on, that you might want to at least provisionally extend the charity with which you regard yourself to some or perhaps most other people.

But the thrust of the utilitarian argument—that we must restrain the viciousness of human nature—rests on an ontological mistake of a sort that we have already seen in its most bloated forms. Utilitarianism in general and this argument in particular seem to be firmly feet-on-the-ground expressions of practical truths: truths of common sense, truths we all recognize: all of us, that is, except idiot idealists like anarchists. But in fact this argument in its most gen-eral form is just another transformation of state power into an idol, into some-thing that transcends the mere human beings who operate it. Otherwise its proponents would understand perfectly well that what they propose is no solu-tion to the problem: to cure people of the selfishness and violence at our heart, we will heavily arm some of them and authorize them to restrain, imprison, or execute others of them. If it is people you are authorizing in this way, you are liable to be merely exacerbating the problem by your own premises. And it would not be crazy to suggest that overall, the people who seek positions of authority that rests on force (we've disposed of consent, recall) will be worse than average in these respects; there will be among them power-hungry, self-aggrandizing martinets. I don't think anyone who's ever dealt with the people who actually rise into police authority will doubt that such things occasionally happen. Ask yourself: who wants a gun and a club and a license to stun, restrain, and intimidate? No doubt, some public-spirited, duty-inspired young men of good character. And some power-obsessed rapists, robbers, and killers. A police force may really keep someone from committing a rape and may arrest a rapist, hence protecting everyone. On the other hand, wherever there is a rape camp, the people who run it are the police.

Worse than this, access to power itself encourages abuse. Controlling oth-ers, enriching oneself, being in a position to do what would amount to a crime if others did it—these can be sources of pleasure and can be addicting. People subject to such addictions are drawn to positions of power and become skilled at the techniques by which it can be gained, for example, simulating an ethic of humility and public service. Indeed, it is customary when acceding to a position of great power to say that one is "humbled," which is more or less laughable. But people can be seduced by the addiction merely in virtue of having access to power, a condition sometimes known as hubris: power breeds arrogance. Power also varies inversely with accountability. To have power yields access to techniques to conceal the real nature of one's activities, and the secrecy of all governments is at least partly intended to carve out a zone of impunity. For such reasons, large concentrations of power seem peculiarly unlikely to have the effect of an overall moral improvement of the species or even of a restraint on criminal activities.

Furthermore, concentrations of power spin off their own prestige or legitimacy. To have power within state-styled concentrations and structures of power yields access to, if not outright control of, the various media of communication. This in turn is in fact always used to bolster the power of the state by controlling the interpretation of its activities, hence reducing its accountability toward zero. The state is among other things about the invention and dissemination of its own legitimacy, both in general and with regard to every specific policy or action. It has had an extensive ability to mobilize people for war, for example, in cases in which the public justification, made possible by the wealth and power of the state, is radically detached from the actual motivation. As Etienne de la Boetie classically argued, the state makes use of the enthusiasm of many people for their own subordination. The tendency of many people to believe that any pervasive, coercive power is legitimate is perhaps not the happiest or most admirable aspect of the human personality.

II

Hume's utilitarian response to social contract theory is straightforward. A social contract only legitimates a state because it is a moral duty to do what we promise to do. But why is it a duty to do what we promise to do? Because the results of a general disintegration of the practice of promising would be disastrous for the happiness of human beings. That is, the moral power of the promise rests on the principle of utility. Since, as Hume argues, the social contract is the merest fiction anyway, we gain nothing by resting state legitimacy on contract. Bentham's statement of the utilitarian justification in "A Fragment on Government" is an underappreciated classic and deserves to be quoted at some length:

> A compact, then, it was said, was made by the King and People: the terms of
> it were to this effect. The People, on their part, promised to the King a general

obedience. The King, on his part, promised to govern the people in such a particular manner always, as should be subservient to their happiness. I insist not on the words: I undertake only for the sense; as far as an imaginary engagement, so loosely and so variously worded by those who have imagined it, is capable of any decided signification. Assuming then, as a general rule, that promises, when made, ought to be observed; and, as a point of fact, that a promise to this effect in particular had been made by the party in question, men were more ready to deem themselves qualified to judge when it was such a promise was broken, than to decide directly and avowedly on the delicate question, when it was that a King acted so far in opposition to the happiness of his people, that it were better no longer to obey him. . . . But, after all, for what reason is it, that men ought to keep their promises? The moment any intelligible reason is given, it is this: that it is for the advantage of society they should keep them; and if they do not, that, as far as punishment will go, they should be made to keep them. It is for the advantage of the whole number that the promises of each individual should be kept: and, rather than they should not be kept, that such individuals as fail to keep them should be punished. This then, and no other, being the reason why men should be made to keep their promises, viz., that it is for the advantage of society that they should, is a reason that may as well be given at once, why Kings, on the one hand, in governing, should in general keep within established Laws, and (to speak universally) abstain from all such measures as tend to the unhappiness of their subjects: and, on the other hand, why subjects should obey Kings as long as they so conduct themselves, and no longer; why they should obey in short so long as the probable mischiefs of obedience are less than the probable mischiefs of resistance: why, in a word, taking the whole body together, it is their duty to obey, just so long as it is their interest, and no longer. This being the case, what need of saying of the one, that he PROMISED so to govern; of the other, that they PROMISED so to obey, when the fact is otherwise?[1]

Bentham specifically credits Hume with decisive objections to contract theory. To Hume must also be attributed the use of utility as a global justification of state power. Notice that Bentham's argument is as likely, or perhaps likelier, to counsel resistance than obedience, and Bentham's brand of utilitarianism would no doubt undermine many actually existing regimes. Hume is of course more "conservative":

The case is precisely the same with the political or civil duty of allegiance as with the natural duties of justice and fidelity. Our primary instincts lead us either to indulge ourselves in unlimited freedom or to seek dominion over

others; and it is reflection only which engages us to sacrifice such strong passions to the interests of peace and public order. A small degree of experience
and observation suffices to teach us that society cannot possibly be maintained
without the authority of magistrates, and that this authority must soon fall
into contempt where exact obedience is not paid to it. The observation of
these general and obvious interests is the source of all allegiance and of that
moral obligation which we attribute to it.[2]

That is, Bentham's position is not a simple legitimation of existing states, but
Hume's appears to be, along Hobbesian lines, though without the distraction
or digression of a contract. It is a matter of the restraint of anarchic passions by
reflection, and the state when thus constituted is analogous to a person. Con-
sumed by passion, a person is power-mad and improvident; restrained by reflection he becomes decent, and happiness is achieved in self-restraint. Analogously,
the people must be restrained by the political leadership, which exercises reason in the political sphere and hence make happiness possible on a social scale.

Whatever Hume may have believed, the utility of state power as a general
matter has always been an open question. It is somewhat difficult, as I have said,
to imagine life without a state. But almost no matter how bad that imagined
anarchic situation might be, we might take a specific historical state and point
out that its results were substantially worse.

Indeed, under the best of circumstances the question is fraught with dif-
ficulties of a kind familiar with regard to all utilitarian ethics: estimating utilities in counterfactual cases or as projected into the indefinite future. With
regard to state power, these questions are especially insoluble, as they seem to
encompass all of history on the widest possible species scale. What would
human history have been like without the invention of the political state?
What will it be like after the political state? What would it be like under this
or that voluntary set of arrangements? These are fully bewildering questions,
and they are not questions that I know how to answer, especially since I am as
subject as anyone to the modern condition of not seeing beyond the state's
horizon. Of course, these calculations need not be a problem if it is tolerably
obvious, as it was to Hobbes or Hume, that the alternatives to state power are
disastrous. Nevertheless, what we do know must make us skeptical about a flat
utilitarian justification of the state.

The twentieth century was the apogee of state power, when every scrap of
land was claimed by some state or other, when the secret police penetrated into
your underwear drawer and armies of hundreds of thousands goose-stepped
proudly in parade, when bureaucracies sucked entire economies into their
ambit, never to be heard of again, not only in communist dictatorships but in

capitalist democracies. And of course the twentieth century was the golden era of war and genocide, beside which the wars of the past looked infantile, like counting coup or mere braggadocio, in which poison gas and atomic clouds wafted hither and yon, and our souls with them, in Hegelian transcendence of the earthly plane.

Wars have been fought along lines that were not state-determined—religious lines, tribal lines, or economic lines—as barbarians migrated away from famines or other barbarians. But the art and technology of warfare was brought to an unprecedented, species-annihilating perfection under the aegis of the political state, with its huge economic resources made possible by coercive taxation, its patriotic scientists, and its ability to disguise from itself and its own people its actual motives.

Here is a summary of the study by Matthew White of the depredations of state powers during the twentieth century: "Because fatality statistics are subject to a great deal of uncertainty in turbulent times, White has opted to conservatism in his reporting of statistics. He also employs a commonly-used statistical stratagem which forces extreme values at the upper and lower ends of the data field to cancel each other out, resulting in a value closer to the probable mean"[a]:

MAJOR MASS KILLINGS OF THE TWENTIETH CENTURY

Rank	Deaths	Event	Time Frame
1	50,000,000	World War II 1937–1945 [Holocaust: 11,000,000]	
2	40,000,000	China: Mao Zedong's regime	1949–1976
3	20,000,000	USSR: Stalin's regime	1924–1953
4	15,000,000	World War I	1914–1918
5	8,800,000	Russian Civil War	1918–1921
6	4,000,000	China: Warlord and Nationalist Era	1917–1937
7	3,000,000	Congo Free State	1900–1908
8	2,800,000	Korean War	1950–1953
9	2,700,000	2nd Indochina War (incl. Laos and Cambodia)	1960–1975
10	2,500,000	Chinese Civil War	1945–1949
12	1,900,000	Second Sudanese Civil War	1983–1999
13	1,700,000	Congolese Civil War	1998–1999
13	1,500,000	Turkish Genocide against Armenia	1915–1923
14	1,000,000	Cambodia: Khmer Rouge regime	1975–1979
15	1,400,000	Afghanistan Civil War	1980–1999
15	1,400,000	Ethiopian Civil Wars	1962–1992
17	1,250,000	Mexican Revolution	1910–1920
18	1,250,000	East Pakistan massacres	1971
19	1,000,000	Iran-Iraq War	1980–1988

Rank	Deaths	Event	Time Frame
19	1,000,000	Nigeria: Biafra	1967–1970
21	800,000	Mozambique Civil War	1976–1992
21	800,000	Rwanda	1994
23	675,000	French-Algerian War	1954–1962
24	600,000	First Indochina War	1945–1954
24	600,000	Angolan Civil War	1975–1994
26	500,000	Indonesia: Massacre of Communists	1965–1967
26	500,000	India-Pakistan Partition	1947
26	500,000	First Sudanese Civil War	1955–1972
30	365,000	Spanish Civil War	1936–1939
??	>350,000	Somalia	1991–1999
??	>400,000	North Korean Communist regime	1948–1999[b]

[my additions]

(?)	400,000	Chechnya	1992–2005
(?)	300,000	Darfur, Sudan	2002–2006

[a] "Mass Deaths and Atrocities of the Twentieth Century," *Wikipedia.*
[b] Matthew White, "Thirty Worst Atrocities of the Twentieth Century,"
http://users.erols.com/mwhite28/atrox.htm

This list, horrendous as it is, is obviously not a utilitarian refutation of all state power. I will insist that large concentrations of state power are a necessary condition of the horrendous wars and genocides of the twentieth century, but they are not sufficient, and it is not the case that all the states of the twentieth century committed genocide, though almost all of them got involved in war, and hence large-scale killing, at some point. But no remotely plausible theory of state power justifies every existing state, and utilitarianism can sort the legitimate from the illegitimate governments on straightforward considerations of utility. On a Benthamite view, according to which a state loses its legitimacy when it becomes a barrier to or a destroyer of human happiness, Nazi Germany, Stalin's Russia, or the Khmer Rouge are simply not legitimate regimes, and, as Bentham explicitly suggests, they ought to be resisted. On the other hand, by a simple utilitarianism, they may very well be legitimate right up to the point when they start gassing people. Or I suppose that a state that is going to have insanely disastrous effects is never legitimate, only it is impossible to know that it is going to have those effects until you and your mother are dead.

Perhaps the state is simply having some growing pains, and once it more or less consolidates into a single international body, as hinted by Habermas, for example, it will be purely devoted to the welfare of all and social justice across the globe—an EU, a UN, a whatever. There is, however, only one way to find out for sure, and that is to put the lives of everyone at stake, to subject everyone equally to the benevolence of a benevolent power that is at every moment almost turning into a raging yet bland and inefficient bureaucracy dedicated unremittingly to species suicide.

III

Rational choice theory, that of James Buchanan, for example, presents itself as a variety of contract theory; the claim is that rational persons would choose to create a certain range of rules and institutions in order to maximize their expected utilities.[3] The argument, in other words, is a hypothetical or idealized utilitarian justification of state power: if there were no state, it would be Pareto-optimal to invent one. Consider two people sharing an island. They settle into what Buchanan calls "anarchistic equilibrium," in which they divide goods and labor according to who can take what from whom and who can protect what from whom. On almost any such distribution, they can both increase their overall utilities by agreeing to a distribution procedure that precludes outright predation or theft. However, each person could maximize his utility by violating the agreement if the other person continued to observe it. In the two-person case, if one person violates the agreement frequently, the other person can be expected to violate it also, and the parties will fall back into anarchistic equilibrium, which hurts them both. In a situation with many parties, one person could opt out of the agreement while others continued to observe it, and it would be to his advantage to do so; since it would be to each person's advantage to do so, the agreement would be unsustainable without enforcement. These are basic insights of game theory in iterated prisoner's dilemma and free-rider situations. To prevent the disintegration of the agreement and its advantages, it will be in the interests of the parties to create an enforcement authority—a minimal state—charged only with the task of enforcing the voluntary agreement.

It is important to see that this is not a contract theory in the classic sense; the question is about what rationally maximizes utilities, which might to some extent explain some of the actual reasons people establish states and observe their rules (though of course the initial extreme abstraction and idealization of conditions should make you wonder whether this has any bite in reality). One way it is different from classical utilitarianism is that it legitimates the state as a result of individual utility-maximizing decisions rather than as a question of sheer greatest good for greatest number. Nevertheless, it is a utilitarian justification of state power. But as these island-dwelling saps think about whether they want to go to the expense of arming a force, building prisons, and so on, they need to think not only about how their utilities will be enhanced by uniform enforcement of the contract, but whether they are preparing their own doom. Even a tiny probability that you will be arbitrarily dispossessed or eradicated in any given moment is hard to put in the balance as you contemplate whether you really want to exit the anarchistic equilibrium. And within a political state, one's continuous vulnerability, one's inability to secure oneself against the overwhelming force, is not necessarily a formula for happiness, though people are amazingly talented at ignoring the threat posed by the state until the moment they no longer exist.

IV

Anybody could design a set of decent institutions. All you have to say is: let our courts of law respect individual rights; let our legislatures be concerned for the common welfare and answerable to the people. Ingenious people, such as those who wrote the American Constitution, might even be able to make some of their ideals practicable to some extent. But framing the thing in this way always performs an abstraction from the realities of the powers thus constituted; such idealisms avert their gaze from the powers they are recognizing or arranging. On any of these views, of course, the state must be invested with a monopoly of coercion resting on deadly force, which is supposed to be not the source of its legitimacy but an effect of it. And once you have invested an actual bunch of people—as opposed to an abstract set of institutions or functions—with a monopoly of force, you are subject to that force.

This force is an always-full reservoir of utilitarian disaster. It may be that the power of some particular state is never turned to genocide or wars of aggression, though there is never power on this scale that is not significantly abused. But if the U.S. government turned on you all of a sudden, took your home and herded your family into a camp, resistance would be ridiculous. The force possessed by this body is absolutely overwhelming, annihilating, and hence it is always potentially your own annihilation. Let the state be as benevolent, as utilitarian, as legitimate as you please, the sheer fact of its overwhelming force is the distant whiff of burning flesh. No force in human history has caused more suffering and death, and one would think that would give practical-but-optimistic utilitarians pause. The power which a utilitarian places in the state to help old folks and poor folks and unlucky folks can always be turned against such folks, or against utilitarians for that matter, and only a fool could examine the history of the twentieth century and not see that once such a power is constituted, all bets are off.

Rational choice theory is another origin myth about the state, wherein we constitute a state so that we can spend more time in constructive, utility-producing pursuits and less time in defensive procedures to keep ourselves and our stuff safe. It does a very plausible job of showing that rational contractors would make this series of choices: (1) recognize the rights of others in exchange for recognition of one's own rights, and (2) undertake some expense in order to ensure this result. However, if the power thus constituted is itself just weapons and money in the hands of a bunch of people, who now represent a standing threat to remove the rights of anyone or who might suddenly explode into a genocidal fury, again all bets are off. And no force can be constituted that is adequate to the task without also constituting an autonomous and irresistible threat to everything it was established to preserve. Rational choice theory cannot possibly support a choice of state power over anarchy.

Obviously, you would tend to opt for a limited state. But any power that is sufficient to protect people from each other is sufficient to be effectively irresistible, and any organization that is effectively irresistible will tend, all things being equal, to become ever-more powerful. Any limited state is a snowball that begins to act in the interest of increasing its own organizational power. With every increase in this power, its ability to increase its power is augmented. That is, the bigger it gets, the bigger it becomes, and so on. I don't think anyone looking with any seriousness at the history of the political state—the history of a state conceived in terms of limited powers as given in a written constitution, such as the U.S. for example—can dismiss this objection as merely conceptual or academic. It may be that some minimal state, a la Nozick, for example, can be justified, and it may well be that it is the only sort of state that can be justified. It might at one point have been possible to institute such a state, though at this point every newly established state would be established out of the wreckage of previous states and would have to be able to resist the incursions of its neighbors. In any case, no minimal state can be restrained from the glorious path to its Hegelian world-historical destiny. By definition state power cannot be contained in the long run, because it must be adequate to impose an effective monopoly of violence.

Look. If you really wanted to maximize happiness in the long run, you would never dangle the blade of the guillotine over your head and hope for the best. Insofar as people are rational, they should live in fear, even amid peace and plenty and democracy, though in normal, nonslaughterhouse, times people are very good at failing to maintain awareness of the threat. The state can kill you in many different ways: by getting your people embroiled in a war featuring hypereffective and refined technologies of death, or by picking you off one by one through application of police power to people of your race, or allatonce in a genocide or atomic vaporization. State power does not always anni- hilate, but once out of a hundred is more than enough to end everyone and everything in the long run. Since, according to its enthusiasts, that is, nearly everyone, state power is inevitable and necessary, and since it cannot be restrained once it is constituted, the long-term utilitarian prospects of our species are extremely poor. They depend on the idea of individual sovereignty coming into currency, on the jealousy with which each person comes to guard her autonomy. If you really think that people are basically greedy and vicious, then the only rational conclusion is that all concentrations of power are dan- gerous, and only complete decentralization to the level of autonomous indi- viduals provides any sort of decent prospects for the long-term survival or happiness of human beings. As long as you believe that people are occasion- ally greedy and vicious, large concentrations of state power can be predicted to have disastrous long-term results.

V

One nice feature of utilitarianism, as one can see beautifully expressed in the work of John Stuart Mill, for example, is that, all things being equal, it must be opposed to force and coercion. Clubbing, torturing, and executing people causes pain, and so is wrong according to any utilitarian, unless the positive effects outweigh that pain. This is one reason that utilitarianism comports fairly well with the basic structures of Lockean liberalism, and it is why utilitarianism and contract theory converge on democracy. Bentham was acutely aware of these facts and proposed a humane reform of all institutions: the schools, the military, health care, and, most famously, the prison.

Bentham's ideal prison, the Panopticon, was designed to absolutely mini- mize the physical pain caused to prisoners and to reduce the pain caused by criminals by reforming them, as opposed to merely punishing them. The Panop- ticon replaces torture with surveillance, or as Bentham put it, the "sentiment of an invisible omniscience."[4] The important thing to know about it is that in it the prisoners are completely visible, available to be seen at all times by the guards. They never know whether they are under active surveillance. Hence they learn to control themselves by internalizing the rules under which they live. Learning to control oneself is cultivating conscience; acquiring conscience reforms the criminal. Punishment before its humane systematization was kind of hit or miss: we had sheriff-type patrols here and there, and if we caught you cutting purses, we might beat you, put you in stocks, or even execute you publicly. By modern standards both apprehension and punishment were impressionistic. In a modern state, there is a schedule of punishments, as well as far larger systems of surveillance, enforcement, and punishment/reformation/treatment.

As Foucault has argued beautifully, this basic approach has been exquisitely expanded and refined ever since Bentham, so that we live in a surveillance society.[5] Under the auspices of compulsory education, richly justified on utilitarian grounds, every child enters the regimes of surveillance early and is formed as a subject by them. This reduces what we moderns might think of as the outright sadism of punishment, and in some ways, on a per-criminal basis as we might say, it reduces the pain involved. To be subject to a modern penal institution, at least ideally, when judged by its own standards, is far less painful than to be manacled to a wall and scourged, for instance. This may be compensated for, however, by the fact that many more people as a percentage of the population are entwined in the penal system, which after all causes considerable suffering simply in virtue of incarceration, and which, of course, is very far from meeting its own humanitarian standards. On the third hand, that may be compensated for by an overall deterrent effect, though I don't think that it could be seriously argued that it has in fact achieved the reformation of criminals on any wide scale.

At any rate, the real question is this: could the manufacturing of subjectivity replace the use of force, or even largely replace it, so that society could be ordered not primarily through direct coercion, but by shaping persons into good citizens? In this case you could have state power without the pervasive use of coercion. To some extent, this has certainly occurred since what Foucault calls the "classical era," circa 1800. One thing we could say is that often the coercive center of state power is shrouded by layers of bureaucratic surveillance techniques, to such an extent that most people in some contexts never come into contact with it at all. A central example would be the bureaucracies of taxation, which proceed through bureaucrats and information systems, with the direct police power lying deep underneath, only accessible in case of egregious defiance. Again, to the extent that this is true, such systems are evidently preferable on utilitarian grounds.

Nevertheless, we are very far from the Foucauldian future in which power circulates, we know not from where. At the heart of every state bureaucracy, force still lurks, and I suggest to you that as long as people consist more or less of animal bodies, they will be sufficiently perverse and recalcitrant to require force if they are to be controlled. More deeply, the idea of a utilitarian utopia that controls everyone while applying deadly force to no one is the deepest sort of nightmare. One way to see this is that it creates the maximum possible threat of utilitarian disaster—a situation in which everyone can be called upon to do anything—the specter of a genocidal machine greater than any achieved up until now. But if in principle it is possible to have a state that does not resort to force, then it is in principle possible for the state to transcend its own essence, shall we say. This remains merely a conceptual worry, and meanwhile we ought to be more focused on the attempt of the state to conceal its own essence in deadly force through the manufacturing of subjectivities and the infinite layering of bureaucracies.

At any rate, we are very far from a state that dispenses with coercion in favor of education and medication, and we'll blow up that bridge when we get to it. Meanwhile, the victory of the utilitarian state and its surveillance bureaucracies has certainly not coincided with a reduction in the deadly force available to or employed by the state. Quite the reverse: in every generation over the last centuries, the state has expanded toward and beyond a power of sheer violence that can consume the world.

chapter four

justicial justifications of state power

I

Another range of possible justifications for state power would rest not on consent or on utility but on considerations of social justice, and specifically on the achievement of a just distribution of social goods and social tasks. A situation of anarchy, according to this view, would be likely to produce intolerable inequalities and oppressions. Plato and Rawls might be mentioned here, and though neither is primarily concerned with the general question of state legitimacy, one might take them to hold the view that states are legitimate to the extent that they are conducive to a just social structure.

It is imperative at this point, however, to sort this justification out from the others. Plato, for example, defines justice as the condition in which all people perform the functions to which they are best-suited, in which each person does her own work.[1] This appears to be an arrangement that is desirable for its own sake. It is truth realized on a social level, an image of the metaphysical structure of the universe on one end and of the individual human soul on the other. Yet throughout *The Republic*, Plato indicates that this arrangement, among all those that are possible, will also make people most happy and prosperous. This may be primarily a rhetorical device aimed at clinching the point with his interlocutors, but to the extent that the position really rests on such grounds, it has been disposed of in the previous chapter. It cannot be seriously asserted that Plato's ideal state—with its rule by lies, its eugenics programs, its infanticide, its structures of absolute authority without recourse—is a reasonable prescription for human happiness. At any rate, for a position to be justicial in the sense I am using it here, it cannot appeal primarily to results understood in terms of happiness.

Likewise, if Rawls's view is in fact, as he sometimes indicates, a social contract theory, then it has already gone the way of all flesh (and, of all theories as well). But Rawls's view is not, I think, a social contract theory; it does not rest the legitimacy of the state on the consent of the governed, though Rawls gesticulates occasionally toward tacit consent. A Rawlsian just social system is justified in virtue of its justice and not by anyone's actual consent to it, though Rawls thinks rational people would consent to it under certain conditions. A social system is just and hence legitimate, for Rawls, apart from the actual consent of any person within it. The contract aspect of Rawls's theory is a heuristic device, not an assertion of self-sovereignty. There is also a rational choice component in Rawls, a la Buchanan, although the conditions under which the choice is made are idealized. To the extent that Rawls is a decision theorist, I have again already treated his view.

It is tempting to have a very short way with justicial views, for some of the objections to the utilitarian standpoint seem doubly apt in this case. Whatever one's conception of justice, actual states might be antithetical to it, and have been. Just as the existence of a state provides a reservoir of utilitarian disaster even in cases where it is, in fact, having good results by utilitarian standards, even a "just state" (the phrase itself is comical) provides a standing threat to justice. Considerable state power will be required in order to realize any particular pattern of distribution. But even if the state does realize a just pattern, the power it embodies can always be turned to the purpose of destroying that pattern. No one is sufficiently asinine to deny that state power has very often been applied unjustly and that any state power is sufficient to be thus applied. Of course, justicial justifications of state power only justify states that do improve distributions of goods from the standpoint of justice, but in all such states, a power is constituted which at any given moment can be turned to unjust purposes. Indeed, state power is characteristically wielded to enrich some and impoverish others.

Plato might have an interesting response to such claims. Justice demands a distribution not only of wealth, but of power itself. A thoroughgoing, indeed totalitarian, state is both the natural and the optimal condition of humankind. When we in modernity talk about "distributive justice," at least on "patterned" conceptions (that is, conceptions that evaluate the justice of a social situation at a certain time by the distributive pattern realized at that moment), we deploy a set of egalitarian presuppositions according to which for some people to have nothing while others are fabulously wealthy, for example, is plainly unjust. A Platonist with regard to justice, however, could hold that an extremely hierarchical distribution of goods could be fully just. The existence of a political power and its hierarchical structure are demands of the world, a reflection of the metaphysical hierarchy of a universe presided over by the Form of the Good. The rule of philosophers would be an image of this structure in the polis.

This is plausible as a justification for state power only if the creation of such states, or some particular creation of some particular states, could be expected to have this result in the long run. In other words, Plato could have argued that political hierarchies always tend toward an ideal condition in which the wise rule, the strong soldier, the clever trade, and so on. In that case, the creation of a state would always, or normally, tend to bring a polis closer to justice. But Plato was a subversive in the Athens of his era, and he thought that the democracy had inverted the proper order of authority, that it amounted to rule by the ignorant. Far from holding that all political power tended to the rule of the wise, he held that even in a case where the wise rule, the state would degenerate through timocracy and oligarchy to democracy and finally tyranny. This was a result precisely of his view that the sensible order failed in its aspiration to emulate the metaphysical order, that the realm of everyday experience was fundamentally false and corrupt. Fending off such a result was to be the task of education and of rule by lies; the only hope for a stable rule by the wise was mind-control on a society-wide scale. If your view of human beings is that jaundiced, there is no reason to expect that any particular constitution will yield a just result, and hence state power cannot be legitimated on such grounds.

On the other hand, there could be a view, and I suppose there have been views, which bite the bullet and say that most hierarchies of political power yield a just result. The clearest examples of such views would be certain tendentious interpretations of the New Testament passage Romans 13:1–4:

> Let every person be subject to the governing authorities. For there is no authority except from God, and those that exist have been instituted by God. Therefore he who resists the authorities resists what God has appointed. . . . For rulers are not a terror to good conduct, but to bad. Would you have no fear of him who is in authority? Then do what is good, and you will receive

his approval, for he is God's servant for your good. But if you do wrong, be afraid, for he does not bear the sword in vain; he is the servant of God to execute his wrath on wrongdoers. (Revised Standard Version)

In such a case one would infer justice from the sheer fact of actuality: power can only be used to do good. Hegel's position might be represented along these lines: whatever the nature of a given state, it is the unstoppable unfolding of God's self-consciousness in world history; stop your bitching. On these views, kleptocracy is as good as democracy, the Killing Fields an expression of the perfect justice of an omnibenevolent and omnipotent deity. No one in her right mind believes such a thing, but one might remark that it not only legitimates the state, it legitimates all successful resistance to the state. It legitimates anarchy as well, once we manage to achieve anarchy. The mandate of heaven is always ultimately demonstrated pragmatically, and the only sensible interpretation of the position is as an affirmation of all actual power relations or any lack thereof that may obtain. It's a kind of political Taoism: an affirmation of all that is. Of course, once you had ecstatically affirmed all that is, you would stop trying to transform everything and everyone by the application of force.

Nevertheless, if we conceive of distributive justice as a matter of a particular pattern of distribution or for that matter a particular procedure for distribution, as Rawls suggests, we are presupposing the need for state power. Rawls, as will be familiar, specifies ideal conditions for the invention of a state: rational people in an original position in which they do not know where they will end up in the distribution of goods. Because they could end up with the worst dispensation, they will, among other things, make certain that the worst postdistribution position is tolerable. Let us suppose that no other values are commensurate with justice or are its competitors. That is, let us suppose that it is never the case that we ought to trade a certain amount of justice for any amount of some other good. This is not necessarily as implausible as it sounds on a Rawls-type view, because justice is a matter of the distribution of other goods. Thus justice is the sum of social goods or the structure in which their role and value becomes comprehensible within an overall scheme. This will immediately entail the necessity of state power, because the distribution of goods cannot be left to chance or to voluntary exchanges or to theft, and so on; there must be a power capable of achieving and preserving a just distribution. It is in this sense that Rawls provides a justicial account of state legitimacy. The necessity of state power flows from the mere idea of justice, or at least from any practical attempt to realize justice in a real scheme of distribution.

An adequate objection to this view cannot be merely that state power can lead to injustice, though few propositions have been more richly or repeatedly confirmed. But whatever the historical realities, state power is conceptually connected with justice, or at a minimum is practically connected with it in every actual case; there can be no justice without an authority capable of distributing and redistributing goods according to a just pattern. Then all the questions would arise not about the legitimacy of the state, but within the presumption of the necessity of the state, as to how much power the state should possess, how this power should be distributed, how the state can be made accountable for the distribution it imposes, and so on. The question of justice, we might say, cannot arise except as a question of how state power is to be applied.

II

Rawls's position is a chimera of social contract and justicial approaches:

> I now turn to one of the principles that applies to individuals, the principle of fairness. I shall try to use this principle to account for all requirements that are obligations as distinct from natural duties. The principle holds that a person is required to do his part as defined by the rules when two conditions are met: first, the institution is just (or fair), . . . and second, one has voluntarily accepted the benefits of the arrangement or taken advantage of the opportunities it offers to further one's interests. The main idea is that when a number of persons engage in a mutually advantageous cooperative venture according to rules, and thus restrict their liberty in ways necessary to yield advantages for all, those who have submitted to these restrictions have a right to similar acquiescence on the part of those who have benefited from their submission. We are not to gain from the cooperative labors of others without doing our fair share.[2]

The contractarian moment here—the "principle of fairness" developed by H. L. A. Hart,[3] which has been devastatingly criticized by Nozick[4]—is massively implausible. As Thoreau said, "Know all men by these presents, that I, Henry Thoreau, do not wish to be regarded as a member of any incorporated society which I have not joined."[5] People benefit all the time from the cooperative efforts of others without thereby obliging themselves to obey whatever rules those others set. Any consumer who uses a product that is better or cheaper than that of a competitor is taking advantage of the cooperative action of the employees of the firm that made the thing. But to say that an obligation to abide by the rules of that corporation was purchased along with the sprocket would simply be bizarre. Or to say that I cannot on some other occasion boycott the corporation, for example, or enter into competition with it, would be puzzling. Probably I am benefiting from the actions of many governments around the world, and perhaps various organized crime syndicates, foundations, football teams, and so on. To say that I am spinning off thousands of obligations in this process is fatuous, particularly in cases where I benefit without any intention to do so or realistic opportunity to withdraw.

On this principle, I am as obligated under the government of a Mussolini as under the government of a Jefferson, and my obligation is undertaken as voluntarily. Furthermore, it would be interesting to try to determine whether the action of some particular government I happen to be under is of *net* benefit to me; on any redistributive scheme, including Rawls's, some people benefit and others pay. Even the question whether anybody, or most people, benefit is an open one, particularly in a case wherein, for example, the state mobilizes for war. Indeed as we go about accidentally and without awareness spinning off obligations willy-nilly, it is certainly true that various of these obligations may be incompatible with one another; a social contract based on this extreme degree of tacit consent to weknownotwhat leaves each person a wretched mass of moral contradictions. Rawls is trying to hold onto the strong intuition that obligations can only be undertaken voluntarily, but honestly, everyone who is not an anarchist will have to let go of that idea completely. Let me just repeat what I said earlier: the low quality of the arguments for state legitimacy is a result of the antecedent credulity, which amounts to groveling, with which the general idea of state power is met by responsible philosophers.

At any rate, Rawls says that even if you benefit from some set of social arrangements, you have no obligation to observe them if they are not just. This indicates that the justice of institutions (as understood, of course, through Rawls's theory) is what fundamentally makes a moral claim to allegiance. Rawls appears to assert this flatly:

> From the standpoint of justice as fairness, a fundamental natural duty is the duty of justice. This duty requires us to support and to comply with just institutions that exist and apply to us. . . . Each is bound to these institutions independent of his voluntary acts, performative or otherwise. Thus even though the principles of natural duty are derived from a contractarian point of view, they do not presuppose an act of consent, express or tacit, or indeed any voluntary act, in order to apply. (Rawls, p. 99)

One comment: even were we to accept the notion that each person is under a moral duty to obey just institutions, this leaves us happily immune from a duty of obedience to any state that has ever existed, or is likely to.

At any rate, it is as a justicial theorist that I would like to understand Rawls; it is only as a justicial theorist that he presents any serious challenge to anarchism as a political philosophy. The details of Rawls's particular theory of justice need not detain us; if you like, I will stipulate that a just social arrangement is classical liberalism, supplemented by some arrangement to enforce a minimum degree of equality in the distribution of goods. Furthermore, it seems likely that a situation of anarchism would substantially violate these principles, though of course the libertarian intuition that drives liberalism also drives some forms of anarchism.

Justicial theorists as a rule make only the most half-hearted attempts to argue for state legitimacy as a general matter. This is in part because state legitimacy follows almost trivially from a justicial orientation. But that in itself shows the conceptual problem. For such theorists, the only real question is what we're going to do with the overwhelming inevitable power that the state wields and how we're going to use it to transform human beings and their social condition. It is, we might say, a technological view in which the transformative power is self-evidently desirable. The state is the only possible machine of global social transformation, and these thinkers, essentially utopian in their outlook, cannot achieve anything of their visionary transformation of all reality without constituting a power sufficient to that transformation.

As Nozick points out with regard to any system of patterned distribution, it will require not only an initial distribution of goods, but continuous intervention in people's voluntary exchanges; obviously that is plenty to give you a powerful state that is coercive by definition of its basic function.[6] (I might point out that Nozick's conception of justice as voluntariness of exchange requires a mechanism for monitoring transactions and adjudicating disputes.) Rawls at least is enough of a modern to try to limit state power constitutionally, but Plato is a straight-up justicial megalomaniac; he envisions a complete transformation of the species achieved by pure repression. In that regard, he shares an outlook with "classical" Marxism. Let me say, or say again, that the justicial position in most of its versions is proudly a priori: it presupposes rather than actually argues for the legitimacy of state power. As an a priori position, no amount of empirical data about the destruction of justice in actual states will count against it.

It is well worth repeating now and then, of course, that any actually constituted state is a threat to justice, however it may be defined. You can treat the state of nature as a hypothetical original position, and you can specify that a constitutional convention establishes a set of just institutions. This does not entail that the actual police and military power that makes the necessary coercion possible will not be turned to unjust ends. To repeat, the objections against utilitarianism are even clearer with regard to justicialism. It is also worth saying that the only hope for a just pattern as understood by Rawls or

Plato is precisely the exercise of a monopoly of coercion resting on deadly force, that is, state power is a necessary condition for social justice as Rawls and Plato understand it.

So this leaves us in a dilemma. State power is the necessary condition of social justice, but it is also the greatest single threat to social justice. This result is almost not empirical; it follows from the definition of justice that entails a pattern of distribution and the constitutive aspect of the state as holding a monopoly of violence. When you constitute a state with sufficient power to achieve a just distribution of goods, you constitute a power with the ability and, admit it, the tendency to commit countless unjust acts, or for that matter with the power and the tendency to impose radically unjust distributions of goods. However, the dilemma is also empirical. Marxists, for example, though they did not often cast their view explicitly in terms of social justice, also advocated patterned distributions. This, they knew, entailed vast applications of state power, which was the source of their disagreement with their anarchist rivals. But the actual distributions achieved by Marxist states have often been extremely unjust (consider, let us say, North Korea), while the machinery of state control has been so coercive as to obliterate the freedom of the people over whom it operated; the former is a predictable, a more or less invariable, result of the latter.

Rawls is no Marxist, of course, and his principles of justice are comparatively gentle. In fact, one way to articulate the dilemma is as a tension between Rawls's two principles of justice: the freedom he values will be vulnerable to the power required to perform and enforce the distribution he recommends. One sees precisely the same tension in his account of state legitimacy (on the pastiche interpretation): he needs to rest it on voluntary acts in order to preserve even minimal liberty in the citizen and to make any wave in the direction of human autonomy before state power. But the bottom line is that he must have state power, either with your enthusiastic participation or over your objections or attempts to withdraw.

The most basic problem is in the gap between the blank happy bureaucratic spread-sheet abstraction of the theory of justice and the way people actually behave when they possess all the weaponry and, with your help, constitute the object of a cult, with all its iconography and pageantry. You can go ahead and specify the precise distribution that would be just, but the people you empower to realize it may use that power in their own self-interest, class interest, race interest, religious interest, or merely to irritate everyone with infinite regulations. And it must be said that justicial views are specifically designed to encourage cults of the state. In Plato and in Rawls, justice is understood as a pattern of distributions of goods and functions. The only thing that can realize this goal, which is nothing less than the comprehensive good or happiness of all humanity, is state power. The state is here cast in the role of redeemer, indeed, our only source of redemption in this world. On a purely justicial view, no violations of the individual rights of citizens (say herding them into cattle cars and dropping them off in mass graves) and no utilitarian disasters (say again the same) have any tendency to show that state power is not justified overall. Although these violations are not compatible with justice (of course, Plato toys with infanticide and so on as strategies of good government), by definition there can be no source of justice but the state. Even if every existing government had degenerated into a tyranny and a war machine—and the historical record is close—we would still go on busily constituting states and handing their representatives the tools and cachet with which to benevolently redistribute the goods or develop atomic weaponry as the case may be.

We ought to consider powers, along with wealth and freedoms, as social goods and as objects of distribution in a Rawlsian-style scheme of justice. Rawls does not explicitly do this, but it is a hard idea to avoid, once it occurs to you, since power is intimately connected with the other social goods, and since the pursuit of power appears to be a feature of rational contractors: it is the kind of thing one would seek to assure oneself of in an original position. If so, the contractors in the original position find themselves in a quandary. To guarantee the minimum acceptable equality of freedom and wealth, they must constitute an extremely effective and dramatic hierarchy of powers. Indeed, there has never been a general asymmetry of human power that can possibly match that which the state deploys by definition. The distributive schemes Rawls calls for can only be achieved by state power, that is, by the monopoly of violence. We might say, roughly, depending on what you mean by *power*, that this entails handing all of it to some folks while stripping it from others entirely. Obviously, this presents a standing threat to the just distributions of all other goods. But if power itself is construed as a basic social good, then Rawls's position is flatly contradictory, because the original contractors cannot guarantee a minimum decent portion of the other social goods to themselves without rendering themselves subject to an abject disempowerment. From this point of view, even accepting more or less all of the assumptions Rawls packs into the original position, it is not clear that the contractors would not choose anarchy, or that they can come up with a scheme that is not internally contradictory.

III

Communitarian political philosophy has been remarkably unconcerned with an account of state legitimacy, and this is revealing. For communitarianism, values and institutions emerge locally and are justified by local practices, by the constituent practices of a community, such as its ideas about membership and autonomy. No global justification of something as general and abstract as "state power" is forthcoming on such a view, though specific states might perhaps be justified in virtue of local values and identities. This seems to be a considerable advantage over the alternatives. Here I briefly consider what a communitarian justification of state power might look like and include it as a foil to Rawls, which is of course one of the ways that communitarians understand their own position. I suppose the justicial category might be a fairly decent fit for communitarianism if the argument is that a state is legitimate insofar as it realizes a conception of justice—or some other central set of values—that emerges from the community it rules.

Communitarian political philosophy has not, again, made it one of its important tasks to give an overall justification of state power, but it has given hints, and there is no doubt what the general approach would be. Michael Sandel says this: "For a society to be a community in this strong sense, community must be constitutive of the shared self-understandings of the participants and embodied in their institutional arrangements."[7] This is a modest or modified Hegelianism, and though I discussed Hegel under the rubric of contract theories, he is of course no contract theorist. Nor does he fit comfortably into the present category of justicial theories. We could perhaps give an Alasdair MacIntyre/Sandel/Charles Taylor (the philosopher, not the criminal against humanity)-style justification along the following lines: justice consists of a set of a set of rational practices by which a community embodies its constitutive values in a scheme of distribution, or a set of distributive principles, or a structure of institutions. We need not add the Hegelian superstructure on which these institutions themselves are the inevitable unfolding of the yackety smackety. Where these values are indeed adequately embodied in a set of state institutions, there the state's power is legitimate. I leave a detailed plausible formulation to advocates of the view.

Communitarianism follows from and implies a vision of human selfhood that traces itself to Aristotle and Hegel, with versions here and there in Wittgenstein and Gadamer, for instance, and which is very elaborately set out by MacIntyre. Sandel's version:

> [W]e cannot regard ourselves as independent [in the way Rawlsian liberalism demands] without great cost to those loyalties and convictions whose moral force consists partly in the fact that living by them is inseparable from understanding ourselves as the particular persons we are—as bearers of this history, as sons and daughters of that revolution, as citizens of this republic. . . . Alle-

giances such as these are more than values I happen to have or aims I "espouse at any given time" [Rawls]. . . . To imagine a person incapable of constitutive attachments such as these is not to conceive an ideally free and rational agent, but to imagine a person wholly without character. (Sandel, p. 179)

I am personally attracted to the organic, historical account of real human groups and practices in communitarian philosophy, and no anarchist short of Max Stirner would object to the idea of community in general. Far from it: we need the idea of community more than any statist. But the reasons we do are revealing. It is ironic that the values in which people's deepest identities consist, the spontaneous values that are made in each community as a rational grappling with its environment, the values that give shape and meaning to the lives of each person, must be enforced with overwhelming weaponry and a gargantuan prison system. To the extent that these values must be imposed and enforced by coercion, they are not the organic values of the community in question. On the contrary, the coercion by which the community's values are impressed upon the bodies of the members of the community is inimical to the status of the group as a community. Where I can behave as a good member of the community—that is, act in accordance with my own deepest identity—or face dispossession and incarceration, there my identity is not articulated in that community, and my values are not reflected in or are not a reflection of that community. More precisely, the question of whether my identity is thus reflected (like the question of whether I consent) cannot arise. Nor does the coercive authority need me to share any particular set of values, though it will possess some power to disseminate whatever values it likes, calling them the organic values of the community.

One possible move here would be to associate state forms with particular communities, so that an Islamic theocracy would be an expression of the community in Iran, a liberal democracy of the United States, a constitutional monarchy of Britain, and an emperor system in China. One thing that we would have to do immediately is point out that all these forms have been imposed not only through an upwelling of community spirit, but also by conquest, so that if we asked the Kurdish population of Iran whether a Shiite theocracy is the expression of their identity, or the Native American population whether they favor majority rule, or the Irish how enthusiastic they are about the Queen, or the people of Tibet whether they think the Chinese Communist Party crystallizes their community values, you might not like the answer. The modern nation-state, that is, fits the communitarian model with extreme imperfection, and relies on crushing and homogenizing rather than expressing and venerating local community traditions. A world of actual communitarian states would have many, many more states than ours does, as well as far, far less coercion.

On the other hand, if we take the fact itself that some state structure does actually rule a given geographical area as evidence that it expresses the indigenous communities of that area, we are back to rank Hegelianism, back to the amazing conclusion that the legitimacy of any given state is established by its actuality. The proper reply to that position is simply to rip the state to shreds—to assassinate its leaders, blow up its buildings, burn its statutes—and then claim the legitimacy of actuality.

There is, of course, a reactionary flavor in some communitarian thought (not that I reject views on the grounds that they are reactionary), and communitarians, above all MacIntyre, often ascribe the overwhelming coercive force of the state to the crisis of identity in modernity. There are certainly more people incarcerated right now than at any time in the history of the world, for example. But that is primarily because in modernity people have become unmoored from their communities, from the values they espouse and the identities they constitute. The diagnosis of modernity is basically early Marx, who frames it in terms of alienation: we are alienated from the organic communities from which we emerged at some point, dehumanized by our economic circumstances. It is very hard to evaluate such claims, and it may be that the small cohesive communities that the communitarians love, especially the Athenian polis, were also extremely alienating in their own way. At any rate, they were certainly capable of producing skeptics about their own way of life, as well as criminals, coups, and decadence. What is ironic would be to say that we have lost our sense of community, our real organic connection with one another; therefore we have to institute a community by coercion. By the communitarians' own standards, a genuine community is not something that can be produced, like a gadget, by social technologies. Their models of communities are not utopias, invented and enforced: indeed it is that tradition that they most explicitly reject. So it would seem that state policies to create communities by coercion are by definition doomed to failure, they would always have precisely the opposite of their intended effect.

There is a slight disingenuousness about communitarianism on such questions. It argues that there is no human selfhood in isolation from a culture, a language, or a set of practices. Then, perhaps, it argues that English should be declared the national language of the United States, a law enforceable by coercive measures. To the extent that a communitarian is not also an anarchist, he in fact regards community not as the ultimate source of values and so on, but as something defined by people with power and imposed by the gun.

IV

A variety of views might make the legitimacy of authority rest not on the legitimacy of rulers or institutions but on the legitimacy of law. At a first stab, one might be worried about whether laws are the sorts of things that can rule or exercise power or however we might phrase this. Laws appear to be texts—either abstract objects or ink stains on pieces of paper. Neither of these seems to be a particularly promising candidate for wielding authority. It strikes me that we should be doubly on guard here for the typical mystifications of power, and that appealing to the legitimacy of the law, not speak of its majesty and so on, is merely an obscuration of the exercise of coercion of human beings by human beings. Whatever may be the rule or authority of law, it seems to depend in the end on the coercive power of some people over others. At least, laws as opposed to rules of thumb, friendly guidelines, or moral injunctions seem to be invariably backed by coercive force; that is, it is at least a necessary condition for something to count as a civil law that it is backed by coercive force. This could make you suspicious that the law is a kind of fog (the squid of state inking the waters of society) between you, the chump—I mean citizen—and the people actually working the coercive machinery.

Perhaps we should be a bit more respectful and circumspect on this matter. It is true that a situation in which the sovereign power rules by a system of laws, where the laws are applied fairly consistently overall (perfection being far too much to ask, as every system of legal administration is distorted by whatever are the power differences among groups), is not precisely the same as one in which the sovereign rules by a series of arbitrary decrees. The basic problem of all coercive states is true here as well: constitute a power that is sufficient for the enforcement of the laws, and you constitute a power that is easily the biggest threat to this enforcement. Even on an everyday basis in societies characterized by the "rule of law," the authorities tend to exempt themselves from their own enforcement. Furthermore, to institute and preserve a system of laws requires actions precisely defined by the law itself as illegal, as in forced taxation (theft), imprisonment (kidnapping), licensing procedures (extortion), slavery (conscription), and so on. Of course, we might say that extortion is different from coerced licensing in virtue of the latter's legitimacy. Given that the actions are otherwise basically indistinguishable, I say: prove it. Or: you're arguing in a self-enclosed and self-serving circle.

A sovereign power in a rule of law is by definition what is not subject to that law, as Hobbes, for example, might have argued. This makes the idea of the "rule of law" appear paradoxical at its heart. Indeed it has suggested to many anarchist thinkers that every assertion of state legitimacy is at its heart paradoxical and that state power always entails a suspension of the moral principles by which it is itself justified. I suggest that the more one reflects on this assertion, the more obvious its truth becomes. Indeed and foundationally, the state authorizes itself to kill and prohibits murder; the state cannot exist except in the midst of this contradiction; the state just is this contradiction. Of course, laws can be rigged up however you like, and I can prohibit you from killing by law while enthusing by law about the technologies of death I wield. I can prohibit theft, then specify procedures by which I can take your stuff. This makes of the rule of law the merest mockery. Well, it is the merest mockery, one way or the other.

Thus one might not really need to get anywhere close to the actual issue of legitimacy, letting the matter rest on the hypocrisy and self-delusion. But let's hit it anyway. One traditional way to put the question would be: what makes a law legitimately coercible? This would be equivalent to the question of state legitimacy if it was essential to state legitimacy that it proceed through such laws, which we may require to be the result of a certain legislative process, to be publicly promulgated, not to be cruel and unusual, and so on, though we must also rig up the laws, or at least the enforcement of the law, so as to exempt the agents of the state in certain systematic ways.

The first traditional answer is provided by positivist legal theory, associated with utilitarianism, which locates the legitimacy of law precisely in force, whereby to say that one should obey the law is simply the prudential dictum that one should avoid punishment. This has the advantage of being hard-nosed and realistic, of not appealing to any occult entities. But it has extreme disadvantages as well. For one thing, as it stands it is circular, and it justifies the coercion on the grounds that it is coercive. Of course one feels that this is no justification at all, and it certainly supports the principle "don't get caught" as much as it supports the dictum "observe the law." Nor is this a mere quibble, as most people do disobey the law and do try not to get caught doing it.

The rival to positivism in the tradition is an Aquinas or Locke natural law theory on which the coercibility of legitimate law is held to rest on the fact that the law has an antecedent moral force and expresses a previously existing moral principle. The basic problem with this view, of course, is that it lends no legitimacy to the laws of states per se, and in fact it is perfectly compatible with—indeed, it entails—holding that we have no duty of any kind to obey an unjust law, which in turn entails that, qua law of a state, the law has no force. Unless sheer submission is itself a natural law (a view that has been assayed more than once), on the most forceful natural law accounts it is not as civic law but as moral law that principles of justice, or reason, or nature, or God address us. It is hard to see how one would carve out exceptions to these principles on behalf of the law of a state; the moral force of the basic principles of morality has nothing to do with their status as civil law. Natural law theory justifies, indeed prescribes, civil disobedience, and the moral legitimacy of civil disobedience entails anarchism, as all its consistent practitioners have understood in their hearts. That is, if you are within your rights, or indeed obliged, to violate laws that in turn violate your conscience, then the law of states has no moral force.

I suppose there are the social constructionist approaches to law which might also have a communitarian flavor. The law on this account has legitimacy as embodying the sense of a community, and its force rests on a kind of conceptual consensus, perhaps one that resides at such a deep level that it does not typically rise to consciousness. Laws are authorized as "forms of life" or are entailed by actually constitutive practices. It is an interesting view because, one would think, it would provide procedures—democratic procedures, surely—by which the moral temperature of the community could be taken. As has been often said, this is a process that becomes more and more difficult as communities become more cosmopolitan. Who has actually participated and who actually agrees or employs the constructions as realities? Not everyone maybe. Dominant groups only, perhaps. At any rate, ask yourself: how can we throw a social construction into question? I suppose the mere fact that we are throwing a social construction into question is a moment in its disintegration as a social construction, since questioning it demonstrates its denaturalization. The very acknowledgment that something is a "mere" social construction is a moment in its disintegration as a social construction. Ask yourself: exactly what do you owe to particular social constructions and the people who construct them? What exactly is the force of any given social construction to bind those who don't already recognize its binding force? What happens when there is a clash of social constructions, as when some people think it's normal or harmless to smoke marijuana, while others think it is sacred to god to smoke marijuana, and still others think such behavior should be punished by lengthy prison terms? This example might make you wonder whether, if we put the legitimacy of the law at the mercy of actual social attitudes or behavior, it in fact has any legitimacy at all, or how, in these circumstances, we could decide which laws have legitimacy. At least it might start you wondering again why forms of life have to be enforced by weapons. In fact, I should think that the status of something as a law shows, in some cases, precisely that there is a problem in the social agreement about it.

We might try to take seriously a Kantian bootstrapping operation in which we derive the legitimacy of the law from the conceptual conditions imposed by the very idea of law. We might assert that the status of any injunction as a law carries with it as a conceptual precondition of universality. You cannot make or acknowledge a law without at the same time admitting or believing or assuming it to be valid for all persons at all times. Of course, as far as that goes, this does not distinguish law from any sort of assertion that puts values into play: judgments of beauty, for example, on Kant's account. Even if we stipulated that law is always universalized in this sense, it certainly does not follow that it is, in fact, legitimate. If this did follow, every single thing that has ever been held to be a law would be legitimate, a conclusion at which even the most dyed-in-the-wool ink worshiper would presumably balk.

V

Habermas's account of legitimacy is, like Rawls's, a chimera of traditional views. Famously, Habermas detects a "legitimation crisis" and seeks a way through and into the future.

> Modern law presents itself as Janus-faced to its addressees: it leaves it up to them which of two possible approaches they want to take to law. Either they can consider legal norms merely as commands, in the sense of factual constraints on their personal scope for action, and take a *strategic* approach to the calculable consequences of rule violations; or they can take a *performative* attitude in which they view norms as valid precepts and comply "out of respect for the law." A legal norm has validity whenever the state guarantees two things: on the one hand, the state ensures average compliance, compelled by sanctions if necessary; on the other hand, it guarantees the institutional preconditions for the legitimate genesis of the norm itself, so that it is always at least possible to comply out of respect for the law.[8]

The first condition is a recapitulation of legal positivism. As such, it perhaps forswears rather than solves the problem of state legitimacy: obviously the fact that a law is actually enforced has no tendency at all to show that its enforcement is legitimate, on pain of endorsing the notion that sheer force makes a moral claim, that you have a duty to do whatever I can force you to do.

The second condition, of course, refers to the procedures by which the law is generated, that is, under conditions of Habermasian communicative rationality, which among other things presupposes universal free participation in the deliberative process. It then becomes possible for each person to regard herself as the author of the law that binds her. This is the social contract element of Habermas's philosophy, but it is perhaps more interesting than Rawls's, which is merely absurd. Habermas's social contract is neither a historical fact nor a conceptual exercise, and it does not rest on a tacit consent of the sort that has

Rawls asserting that everyone has always already agreed to virtually anything. The Habermasian contract is a process and an aspiration; ideal communicative conditions or democratic deliberative institutions are something that we strive for and that in the long run we hope to approximate. That, I must say, is a remarkably decent point of view, and it seems to emerge from a critique of actual power relations rather than a mere attempt to rationalize existing forms of subordination.

It is worth emphasizing, however, that it remains a mere aspiration. Indeed, I don't think any state has ever been able to meet even Habermas's first condition: no state has been able assure average compliance with its laws. Lawbreaking is typical in every state, if nothing else because, as states go on, their laws swarm like mosquitoes. But it would be a more serious objection to say that no state has achieved a deliberative process that is anywhere close to meeting Habermas's conditions on legitimacy, in which factors such as wealth, race, citizenship status, and so on are irrelevant to political participation. The idea that any existing regime approximates that condition is false on its face.

It is not ridiculous to think that there could be a good theory of the legitimacy of the state according to which it is possible for a state to be legitimate but according to which no state that has ever existed has actually been legitimate. This, of course, is a position that might lend some comfort to anarchists, especially to the extent that a realization of the conditions of legitimacy was seen to be in practice extremely unlikely. Then again, anarchism itself is extremely unlikely.

Nevertheless, Habermas's theory is not plausible. The very nub of it is the notion that each person can conceive herself to be the author of the laws that bind her: "From the standpoint of *legal theory*, the modern legal order can draw its legitimacy only from the idea of self-determination: citizens should always be able to understand themselves also as authors of the law to which they are subject as addressees" (Habermas, p. 449). After hundreds of pages devoted to such topics, I yank my gaze from Habermas's text unsure about whether he is asserting that each person must actually be the author of the laws that bind her or that she must believe of herself that she is their author. I suggest that fatal problems lurk on either side.

The sense in which each person in any state is the author of its laws is peculiar and highly attenuated, even where perfect communicative conditions have been achieved. It sounds like she drafted the laws, made them up and wrote them down, and it gets its little whiff of liberty from this basic meaning of the term *authorship*. Indeed, who wouldn't be satisfied to be the lawgiver for oneself (though I reserve veto power)? This amounts simply to self-sovereignty, that is, to anarchy. Or it may be taken to mean that one really consents to the laws, which is of course false under any possible deliberative process short of the sudden unexpected ontological transformation of our species: the emergence of a general will that is also an annihilation of all individual wills. Or it could mean that one roughly agrees to the conditions of deliberation, which one must, ultimately, due to the fact that one is the sort of creature that can engage in communication, and hence in some implicit way to its results. This appears to be what Habermas means, of course. To call this "authorship" seems a trifle disingenuous.

I get the feeling, however, that his authorship is a fiction, precisely because every formulation deflects the question. One could put it less pejoratively and say that it is a state of mind or a phenomenological event: one really does forge a general will by forming the impression of a unanimity. You must *be able to regard yourself* as the author of the laws, even though you are (of course!) not their author at all. Among its many other problems, for example that it appears merely to be the inculcation of a delusion of some kind, such an impression or feeling of unanimity is something that has cursed our species. It is at the center both of totalitarian political theory and of real genocides. If it is not supposed to be based in actual self-sovereignty, it merely serves the purposes of power.

It is, as it were, at this crossroads with totalitarianism that Habermas mutates from a kind of visionary of democracy to a spokesman for a truly chilling vision: a world state governed by a rational and indefinitely large bureaucracy. Once everyone regards themselves as the author of the shelves of regulations imposed by this bureaucracy (for which, in Habermas, the European Union is the model), then acquiescing in them all, including those one reviles and rejects, is an expression of one's autonomy. You are the FCC, the FDA, the DEA, the DHS, the NSA of yourself. You the author of the wars you regard as unjust; you love what you hate, accept the principles you violate, create what disgusts, imprisons, or beats you. You are the author, in short, of your own degradation.

V

One very clearly justicial account of state legitimacy—and the most plausible account I have seen—is sketched by Randy Barnett in *Restoring the Lost Constitution*. It rests on a conception of inherent rights but is not a contract theory, a disarming approach, at least to me. First of all, Barnett gives an extremely clear statement of the paradoxically totalitarian implications of social contract theory:

The fiction of popular sovereignty becomes dangerous when legislatures are conceived of as a surrogate for "We the People" themselves. Because "the People" can "consent" to alienate [almost] any particular liberty or right . . . legislatures, as the people's surrogate, can restrict almost any liberty and justify it in the name of "popular consent." In short, if legislatures literally "represent" the people, then anything the legislature "consents" to is consented to by the people as well. This means the fiction of popular sovereignty allows a legislature to justifiably do anything it wills.[9]

We have already seen ample reason to believe that all the scare-quoting is justified. Because Barnett is a believer in natural or inherent rights and regards the state as instituted to preserve such rights—a basic tenet of Lockean and Madisonian democracy—and because he regards the fiction of consent as a totalitarian moment, he detaches the natural rights from the social contract aspects of democratic political theory.

Barnett's strategy for legitimation also rests on legitimating the law rather than the state per se. At any rate, here is the nut: "[A] law is *just* and therefore binding in conscience [hence, legitimately coercible], if its restrictions are (1) *necessary* to protect the rights of others and (2) *proper* insofar as they do not violate the preexisting rights of the persons on whom they are imposed" (Barnett, p. 44). Framing the theory in terms of necessity and propriety, a felicitous idea in itself, is intended to connect the view to the "sweeping" clause of the U.S. Constitution, which gives the Congress the power "to make all laws which shall be necessary and proper for carrying into Execution the foregoing powers, and all other Powers vested by this Constitution in the Government of the United States, or in any Department of Officer thereof" (Article 1, Section 8). So among other things Barnett's account of legitimacy for law is intended as a (libertarian) reinterpretation of the Constitution. He continues:

The second of these requirements dispenses with the need to obtain the consent of the person on whom a law is imposed. After all, if a law has not violated a person's rights (whatever these rights may be), then that person need not consent to it. The first requirement supplies the element of obligation. If a law is necessary to protect the rights of others (again, whatever these rights may be), then it is obligatory for the person on whom it is enforced as protecting that person's rights is obligatory on the legal system itself. Persons have an obligation to obey such a law just as they have an obligation to respect the rights of others. (Barnett, pp. 44–45)

This account of course rests on the presumption that the idea of natural rights can be made good, but I do not reject it on those grounds; I am, like many anarchists, at least provisionally sympathetic to the idea of natural rights.

A few things to notice. First, the view does not rest the legitimacy of a law on its being the law *of a state*, for example, on its having been passed by a legislature or proclaimed by a sovereign. The obligation we are under to obey laws that meet Barnett's standards are obligations we would, on his natural rights presumption, be under to obey any set of rules, violations of which would compromise people's inherent rights. That is what we should expect to emerge from the natural rights tradition with which Barnett identifies himself. In that sense, this is no argument for state legitimacy, though it is compatible with state legitimacy insofar as a state limits itself to the functions prescribed in the principles of necessity and propriety, or rather, limits itself to activities that are compatible with these principles.

These limitations, however, are extremely stringent, and no existing state is anywhere near meeting them: every existing state employs coercion in ways incompatible with these principles. That should begin to make you wonder whether such principles are of any practical moment with regard to state power. This might again be framed as the sort of argument I turned against utilitarian accounts of legitimacy: actual states, far from helping us achieve the sort of justice Barnett envisions, are the most massive violators of it, and constituting a power capable of coercing obedience to legitimate laws is also constituting a power capable of coercing obedience to arbitrary will, or massive violations of the natural rights of some group, or of everyone. Given that no state has ever for a moment observed the limits Barnett imposes, it is not clear that as a rule state power is justicially preferable to anarchy on Barnett's account. This is a conclusion to which Barnett might happily agree.

The sort of state legitimated on Barnett's view, if any, is what has been termed "minarchist"; Nozick is a proponent of a similar structure. The justification of state power rests on its extreme minimalism. It is not even clear that there can be a state that observes these limits. Show me a state, for example, that does not confiscate people's property or regulate its media and economy. These functions are (often) incompatible with legitimacy on Barnett's view. That view has this in common with the social contract theory it rejects: it legitimates the state to the extent that the state approaches a condition of anarchy. Indeed, we have seen this a number of times with regard to a number of points of view, enough to propose it as an axiom: The greater the power of the state that is legitimated on any account of state legitimacy above a certain tiny minimum, the less plausible that view is. This is true even of the util-

itarian justifications, because the more power one constitutes, the more poten-
tial there is for death and destruction. It is true with regard to communitarianism, true according to any view that requires consent, true on any view that
demands justice. That all these accounts in their most plausible forms keep
pulling you back away from state power is interesting. State power can plausibly be held to be legitimate only in tiny quantities. In the constitution of all
actual states, these quantities have been massively exceeded, and no state can
be constrained to observe them.

CONCLUSION OF PART II

The attempt to justify state power ethically has made no substantial progress for
centuries. Indeed, for two hundred years, philosophers have rested content with
recapitulating Hegel, Locke, or Hume, or constructing collages, such as those
of Rawls and Habermas. Of course, probably the best policy is to approach the
monuments of the intellectual tradition in a posture of respect, with a presumption that they were produced by smart people thinking hard and so cannot be merely ridiculous. With regard to the arguments that have been offered
for the legitimacy of the state, I cannot manage to assume this posture. The
arguments themselves are pitiful—riddled with holes, rationalizations, and
dreams of submission dressed in the leering semblance of rationality.

And whatever you may think of the motivations, the arguments themselves
are shockingly fallacious. One strives by any means to justify the central moral
fact of one's life: one's destruction as an autonomous human being; one's pervasive use for the purposes of others; one's tininess, impotence, and one's collusion in this tininess and impotence; one's need for it, love of it. One is an
insect by choice, by commitment, by history, by necessity, though hardly by
philosophy. And when it comes time to argue, one argues as an insect would
argue. One philosophizes like a gnat.

"Locke," "Rousseau," "Hegel," "Habermas" are sounds that reverberate
through human history like the tolling of great big bells. They have their
moments: Locke's epistemology, Rousseau's philosophy of education, the
very idea of the philosophy of history, the lovely dancing delight that is the
prose style of Jurgen Habermas. But their books are also all contained within
the still-emerging world-historical destiny of the state, not to speak of its
patronage systems and threats of repression. There may be better justifications of the existence of the state than they came up with, but any candidate

had better start more skeptically, by feeling actually threatened and undermined by anarchism. So we anarchists must do all we can to destroy their arguments and any others that may eventually be put forward. Only thus can we serve the cause to which we are all, ultimately, committed: the destruction of human moral autonomy.

part III

toward
something
else

chapter five

silhouette of an anarchism

In political philosophy, sheer destruction is necessary and beautiful. But starting with my mom, people are always pressing me to articulate some positive vision of the polis, as though blowing shit up wasn't a task to occupy a productive lifetime. At any rate, I do intend to develop a history of a certain sort of individualist anarchism and a set of guidelines that will enable future generations to answer their most pressing question: what did Sartwell think we should do? That will be another book, bigger than this one and less annoying. Meanwhile, having cleared the world of its existing states, I just want to sketch my vision of where we go from here.

I aspire to an anarchism that:

(1) rests on the idea that each person is the owner of herself, or is self-sovereign;

(2) takes the individual human body to be the primary location of consciousness, identity, decision, and responsibility;

(3) is fundamentally nominalist with regard to collective entities such as peoples, classes, nations, institutions, families, and so on and thus seeks to explain the action of such entities by appeal to the states and transformations of the individuals out of which they are composed;

(4) does not regard human beings as merely self-interested or incapable of altruism;

(5) does not regard human beings exclusively in their economic aspect and does not seek to reduce human action to a single dimension of causation, but rather to recognize a plurality of personalities and motives;

(6) emphasizes the connection of the individual to other persons as constitutive of individuality, but asserts that an affirmation of individuality is the first moment in re-establishing this connection;

(7) emphasizes the connection of the individual to the order of nature—to nonhuman creatures and inanimate objects—and its constitution out of such relations;

(8) is not an amoralism or an immoralism or a libertinism but is compatible with and encourages conscience and self-discipline;

(9) does not prescribe any particular set of social arrangements but leaves such arrangements to the voluntary decisions of individuals.

The content of these ideas is best left to a discussion of their history, of which I intend to write some version as the years stretch into decades. Nevertheless, some clarification is in order. Let me precede that, however, with a brief discussion of my strategy in arguing about moral norms.

I do not have a well worked-out metaethical theory, that is, a theory about the ground of moral claims and a general strategy for establishing such claims. I am not even sure whether such a theory should be teleological or deontological, though I tend habitually toward the latter, and I believe that to be adequate to widely-shared moral intuitions, a moral theory would have to use both criteria. This makes it sound like I am an "intuitionist," and I am willing to accept that label to the extent that it means I think fundamental moral intuitions do not admit of and do not require rational underpinnings or reduction to a single principle or dimension of evaluation. Such a position foregoes any pretense that it can demonstrate its truth to those who disagree, or even have any real leverage in persuasion. My claims, then, will be convincing—even provisionally as being the sorts of things that *could* be convincing—only to people who share certain fundamental intuitions. This is important, however, as being an application of the individualism I endorse. I do not seek to constrain you to believe (though I'm not above a bit of brow-beating, as you know if you've made it this far): I ask you whether you do not agree. My basic strategy is fundamental to my ethical stance itself: I assume that certain features of the way I understand myself are common to the self-understandings of others, and I ask that we resolve to accord to others the rights or the understandings that we extend to ourselves. For example, I have no knock-down argument that recreational torture—torture for the sheer enjoyment of it—is wrong. But I do not want to be tortured. I assume that you feel the same. And if you do, then I ask you to join me in condemning torture when it is performed on people other than ourselves as well.

Specifically, I do not want to proceed on the assumption of my own superiority to other people, though obviously I'm superior to you or I'd be reading your book. I do not want to assume that whereas, for example, I can control my own behavior in some respect, you cannot. I do not want to assume that while I would not start pillaging if there were no policemen, you would. It's not that I am asserting that I am an exemplary person and so I assume everyone else is; I am assuming not only that there are certain moral intuitions that are widely shared but also that I am, on average, no better or worse than other people in the dimensions picked out by those intuitions. Arguments in political philosophy too often are explicitly elitist: they assert that while, of course, people like us are trustworthy free men, people like them must be continuously restrained. At any rate, there is a universalizing move implicit in what I'm saying, which may be no more than the golden rule extended as a strategy for achieving moral understanding of others through examination of ourselves. I daresay such an idea is conceptually problematic, and I admit that I can't show that it's true or preferable to other moral stances or standards. But I ask whether you share this point of view, or whether you want to share it. If you do, we can at least keep talking. Now on to the basic aspects of an anarchism.

(1) *An anarchism that rests on the idea that each person is the owner of herself, or is self-sovereign.*

The idea of self-sovereignty does not necessarily have to be accounted for in terms of ownership, as I have done above, and admittedly the idea that each person is the property of herself has the ring of paradox or tautology. Specifically, the idea of self-sovereignty develops out of early nineteenth-century antislavery thought, in which it is a way of attacking the idea that it is possible to own other people. The idea that people can be owned reduces people to the status of mere things or destroys the moral claim that they make as human beings or as whatever sort of things count morally. That is why people such as William Lloyd Garrison and John Brown held slavery to be the sum of all sins—not merely something bad but the very emblem and essence of evil.

One way to put the idea is that each person is the sole owner of herself. This is to affirm, first, that I have a fundamental right to dispose of myself as I see fit. I conceive this to be as fundamentally incompatible with state power as it is with slavery. The idea of self-sovereignty affirms that there is a region of autonomy around each person that it is wrong to violate. It is not only those who advocate slavery who deny this view; various forms of collectivism do not take individual persons seriously as making a moral claim and seek to operate over persons at the level of groups, races, genders, classes, nations, and so on. The result of such procedures is, precisely, slavery; they reduce individual persons to chattel, or do not take seriously any claim they may make to autonomy, on grounds that might be called ontological: they do not in some sense believe in the existence of individual persons, or perhaps they regard individual human persons as mere epiphenomena of capitalism or something.

This idea, I believe, can be refuted by the demand for honest introspection. Indeed, since it is incompatible with the very idea of introspection, it will not survive this process even momentarily. I would ask Chairman Mao, for instance, whether he believes himself to be the center of his own consciousness, or whether he, himself, would feel violated by being led off in chains and forced to work in the fields twelve hours a day. Is it he who writes, who rules, who sees the red flag? Is it he who lusts, who swims the Yellow River, who shakes the hand of Nixon? Or is it a class, a people, the spirit of a time? If he answers in terms of collective entities, those of "Marxism-Leninism," for example, I suggest to you that this is simple mental illness, which in this case leads to massive slaughter. In Mao's imagination, the individuals he expunges have no reality. They are a kind of mass of stuff, as he is the embodiment of the future; everyone involved is relieved of their individuality and can then be removed from this earth without harm to anyone.

One cure for people who sincerely decenter consciousness into collective entities, and hence do not take individual autonomy seriously, would be to subject the proponent to physical pain. Now: who is having this pain? What is it like to have this pain? Where is this pain? That the individual body is the locus of pain is enough, at any rate for the consciousness associated with that body, to want the pain to stop, to demand that, if someone is causing it, that they cease, and so on, while other bodies sharing your class consciousness are not aware of it at all. Bill Clinton may have felt your pain, but there he was on television, smiling as you writhed.

If a philosophy does not take the autonomy (or for that matter the pain) of each person seriously and does not take it as fundamental, I believe that, as the product of an individual consciousness, it is hypocritical. But further I believe it to be a conceptual genocide; it justifies murder, or rather denies the very possibility of murder, since killing individual human bodies is killing things that have no real or independent existence, much like killing bees for the sake of the hive or amputating limbs for the sake of the body.

One might call this ethical emphasis on individuality and autonomy Kantian. I am not trying to deduce it transcendentally, however, but through an examination of the reality of what happens when we cease to take the autonomy of persons seriously, and the reality of what you yourself feel and believe when your autonomy is violated in ways of which you become conscious. The most radical abolitionists, Henry Wright and Nathaniel Rogers, for example, held that human governments which rested on coercion claimed ownership in persons and were, in the precise and literal meaning of the term, slave masters.

(2) *An anarchism that takes the individual human body to be the primary location of consciousness, identity, decision, and responsibility.*

This follows essentially from (1) or perhaps (1) follows from it. There are various ways in which consciousnesses can come into alignment; indeed, communication might be defined as the sharing of consciousness, and certain intense collective experiences yield the sensation that one's consciousness is lost, generalized, or merged with others. Nevertheless, consciousnesses are fundamentally detached from one another to more or less precisely the degree that human bodies are detached from one another, though of course human bodies join one another in various ways on various occasions. This is even inscribed in the language we use to describe moments or dimensions in which consciousness seems to become shared or collectively embodied. Communication, like perception, is essentially a physical transaction by which bodies penetrate one another. But the permeability of bodies hardly shows that they have no reality: quite the contrary. Even the very idea that we can communicate with one another supposes that we are separable from one another, that our identities are distinguishable, even if put at stake in the very act of communication.

Responsibility, we might say, is correlated with autonomy or is identical with it. The fact of our responsibility is the fact of our autonomy; this is not primarily an assertion of what should be but of what is the case. One of the problems with, say, Maoist collectivism and with chattel slavery, is that they are incompatible with the autonomy of persons. Viewed from another side, they are incompatible with moral responsibility because they make the subject of responsibility into a fantastic something-or-other, as Kierkegaard would put it, thinking of Hegel's view of history. A theory on which there is no autonomy or on which identity inheres fundamentally in classes, nations, races, genders, or communities—or in general views that enthuse about the social construction of the self—provides a universal excuse. That I treat you as a mere thing or that I kill you neither violates anyone's autonomy, since there is no such thing as individual autonomy, nor renders me guilty of anything, since I am not fundamentally the agent that acts. A principle acts, or a group acts, or the world acts, or history acts, and the fact that I pull the trigger and you end up in a shallow grave is neither here nor there. This is actually the most severe moral problem of this age, in which huge bodies of people form up into killing machines and in which the individuals involved are specifically released from moral responsibility for what they do.

Indeed, this we may say is the moral essence of the state and perhaps really its ultimate purpose: to form people up, or ball them up into something, to homogenize them or blend them into a single body—the Leviathan, body politic, or general will—mashing people like potatoes for the purpose of relieving everyone of responsibility for the killing, the robbery, the extortion, the kidnapping. The state must be understood primarily as a fantastic collective agent that relieves the soldier, the judge, and the bureaucrat of responsibility for whatever can be understood to be an official function. The state is a mechanism for the fantastic reconstruction of human beings into things, that is, objects with no agency, no autonomy, and no responsibility.

At the war crimes or crimes against humanity trial there is only one defense: it wasn't me, it wasn't even us, it was the functioning of this giant machine. I was obeying orders. This excuse, I propose to you, is always worth absolutely nothing; it rests on an ontological mistake: the state's self-understanding as a transcendent being that is capable of expunging or liquidating persons into sheer functions. That, I repeat, is what the state is for. It is at its heart a mere, though complete and universal, moral excuse. I assert that this result follows on every single justification of state power and is more than sufficient in itself to constitute a moral refutation of the entire project. Obviously, this isn't some sort of merely academic point in political theory.

(3) *An anarchism that is fundamentally nominalist with regard to collective entities such as peoples, classes, nations, institutions, families, and so on and thus seeks to explain the action of such entities by appeal to the states and transformations of the individuals out of which they are composed.*

Of course, I continue to use the terms that pick out the abstractions or phantasms I seem to reject: *state, government, army*, and so on. Though terms like these are problematic in the sense that one gets the funny feeling that they could turn out to be meaningless, they are not going anywhere and are fairly essential to continued communication or at least continued political theory. At any rate, if one is concerned at all with a semblance or a sliver of autonomy and responsibility, if one actually believes of oneself that one exists, one had better scout a nominalism with regard to these entities or prepare to acknowledge that one has already been expunged. These things are, on the account of their fans, Platonic—the eternal abstract indestructible concepts that account for the reality we can perceive: the most real things, the only objects of knowledge: the truth.

With regard to his Forms, Plato went ahead and drew the conclusion that this world is a mere illusion, and there is no such thing as the human body.

At any rate, I think simple humanity and decency would indicate that we should take an approach like this: an army consists without remainder—is nothing but and can be reduced conceptually to—individual human beings and inanimate objects such as buildings, missiles, uniforms, and so on. Of course we face a ship of Theseus sort of problem because the actual set of things that comprise an army shifts with time, while the army remains the very same army it was. Thus, we would have to specify identity conditions conceived as a specification of the sort of transformations that something could undergo and remain "the same" army that it was to begin with. But the alternative would seem to be that the army is not composed of human beings and inanimate objects, but is an ideal, a persisting independently existing object separable from its physical components. It might be possible to make such an account coherent and even to acknowledge, on it, the real-world manifestations of the army, its component human beings and textile goods, for instance. However, the moral and political implications of such an approach are intolerable, just as the moral and political implications of Platonism were intolerable. Wherever there is an institution, one should identify it as, and explain its procedures by reference to, the persons and objects that compose it. Either that or one should expunge oneself into it, become oneself an abstract bit of an abstract object.

Puzzles about the ontology of the state, specifically about its ontological self-presentation, have motivated the persistent and otherwise puzzling claim that the state does not exist at all. Nietzsche and Thoreau, for example, have expressed such skepticism. Thoreau writes:

> To one who habitually endeavors to contemplate the true nature of things, the political state can hardly be said to have any existence whatever. It is unreal, incredible, and insignificant to him, and for him to endeavor to extract the truth from such lean material is like making sugar from linen rags, when sugar-cane may be had.[1]

Or in the annoyingly oracular words of Nietzsche's Zarathustra, who despite his ancientness seems to be attacking Hegel:

> [W]hatever [the state] says it lies—and whatever it has it has stolen. Everything about it is false: it bites with stolen teeth, and bites easily. Even its entrails are false. Confusion of tongues of good and evil: this sign I give you as a sign of the state. Verily this sign signifies the will to death. Verily, it beckons to the preachers of death.[2]

This denial of the state's existence is the correlate of the history, which I traced above with regard to the outcome of social contract theory, of the continual ontological apotheosis which the state has been achieving in the minds of its enthusiasts. If the reality of state power tends to generate anarchists, the ontological self-promotion of the state generates skeptics about its actual existence. The state in modernity rests on a lie, the sort of lie that is at its most absurd and obvious in Hegel, and then it spins off hundreds of lies per second; it insulates itself from and purports to manufacture the truth. Its power by its own account is a power to transform reality in any way it sees fit; it comes to claim an omnipotence. But even as it is remaking reality by means of its epistemic insulation, its secrecy, its gigantic propaganda machine, its educational systems, and its access to or control of all media, it is making itself ridiculous and displaying its futility. In its ridiculous humanity, the state is a parody of its self-understanding.

(4) *An anarchism that does not regard human beings as merely self-interested or incapable of altruism.*

Notoriously, apparent acts of extraordinary altruism or everyday generosity can often be accounted as proceeding from disguised self-interest, and often such an account is plausible. But that real generosity is impossible is, I suggest, constantly contradicted in our experience. Only a pre-existing theoretical perspective— perhaps a kind of Darwinism, an odd notion of practical rationality, or economic determinism—would cause you to deny this when your experience confirms it. (I should say: I hope your experience confirms it.) At any rate, as I have said already, I do not intend to rest my anarchism on the natural benevolence of human beings, and I believe that if people were always out only for themselves and were willing to lie, cheat, steal, and kill under any circumstances to further their own interests, this fact would have no tendency to support a statist political philosophy, but rather a tendency to refute it. However, my view, for which I can provide no decisive arguments, obviously, is that we are a mixed bag and that any plausible political philosophy has to acknowledge that fact and be reasonable under conditions of either competition for scarce resources or cooperation for shared goals (not that these two circumstances are mutually exclusive). I specifically want to differentiate my version of individualism from various sorts of egoism: metaphysical, psychological, economic, and moral.

A central question in political philosophy is: what sort of situation is likeliest to encourage generosity and other qualities of character that we admire? One justification of the political state would certainly be that it is, as it were, a congealed generosity in its function of redistributing wealth and providing for the safety and welfare of its citizenry. This could be represented as a matter of the overall utility of the society or as a matter of the virtue of the citizens. As a question of utility, we have already dealt with it, but in terms of virtue the results are obvious. If the redistribution is imposed by coercion, it says nothing about the virtue of the people from whom wealth is redistributed. Rather, the expression of their virtues would be constricted by the confiscation of their wealth. Of course this might be the only hope for certain people's survival or the only chance for people to live a decent life. That is a question about the actual effects of state authority on the welfare of its citizenry. But just as your state has the effect of reducing or alleviating entirely your responsibility for your actions, it also alleviates your responsibility for generosity: the more coercion, other things being equal, the less virtue.

One question that an anarchist should face as squarely as possible is whether and how severe inequalities of any kind could be ameliorated without the application of state power. One might even put this as the question of justice: what, if anything, is justice for an anarchist, and how can it be achieved under anarchist assumptions? We have seen reasons to believe that "patterned" accounts of justice in distributions more or less conceptually require sufficient coercive power to achieve substantial redistributions and to prohibit certain kinds of transactions. Such accounts are of course incompatible with anarchism, but that makes it seem that anarchism is compatible with extreme injustice in the patterned sense, or extreme inequalities of wealth, or access to the exercise of rights.

One way to begin to address this problem is to ask seriously whether the state does, usually does, or ever does have the overall effect of increasing justice in these senses. It is obvious that for the most part state power is used for the benefit of those who wield it, or for the benefit of those with enough power to control it, and plenty of anarchists have argued that an increase in state power is invariably accompanied by increases in inequality. This is plainly true if the question is about inequalities of power; in anarchism there is no mechanism of power comparable to the state and hence no inequality of power of the vast extent typical of state-ridden societies. But it is just as true that most states do engage in redistributive activities, even if state power is what ultimately makes possible the great concentrations of wealth and power that it then seeks to some extent to ameliorate.

The question of justice is an embarrassing one for anarchists, precisely because we are prohibited by our own view from designing an ideal pattern of distributions; our position is that utopian or ideological design is a problem, not the solution. One way to address this problem would be to develop a theory of justice that emerges from or is fully compatible with anarchism. This, I suggest, is not the right move and cannot be accomplished in an interesting or responsible way. Indeed, it is not too much to say that when anarchists have addressed the question of justice, they have resolved it into a question of freedom. If they talk about equality, it is equality in freedom or equality of rights. But to say that justice simply is freedom does not do a particularly good job of capturing the ordinary-language sense of the term. Of course the question of inequality in distribution could always be raised in different terms.

Another possibility is to reject the very idea of justice as somehow misleading. I am tempted by this approach, especially as regards questions of distributive justice. I often feel that I have a pretty direct intuitive grasp of value-terms, even such nasty thickets as *beauty*. But *justice* seems interminable to me at many points. I am tempted to define almost any term, but defining *justice* seems to me useless or impossible. At any rate, it would not be implausible to hold that it is conceptually a statist term, and for an anarchist simply to abandon it on those grounds. For example, the concept of "criminal justice" is surely one that only makes sense on the presumption of the existence and legitimacy of the state. A criminal, in any decent or literal sense, is someone who violates an actual law; a law is a rule of behavior promulgated by a state; the procedures of criminal justice with regard to a determination of guilt and punishment presuppose a state apparatus. And distributive justice, as we have seen, tends to bring with it a similar set of presumptions: that there are people with the power to describe and ameliorate distributions on a society-wide scale.

But mere skepticism with regard to justice will open anarchists to the perfectly serious charge that they simply countenance extreme inequality of wealth, terrible acts that would be criminal were there any law, and so on. You can call these questions about justice or not, but still they are questions.

Here I think an anarchist cannot deflect the obligation to speculate, to design, and to hope. My own hope proceeds through ideas such as Josiah Warren's principles of the cost limit of price and labor exchanges, for example, and Proudhon's mutual banks and voluntary federations, or the understandings of Voltairine de Cleyre about what a criminal is and how criminals should be treated. That is, I can specify an anarchist situation that I would regard as fundamentally just. Here, it is true, anarchism becomes utopian. Perhaps it also becomes deeply unrealistic, though I hope at some date to give some reasons to think that some aspects of the program are possible to accomplish. But the very idea of justice, I suppose, is utopian in its essence, and if we do not simply jettison it, we have to start saying something that captures a set of positive values.

There could, I acknowledge, be a situation in which there was no state that was extremely unjust by any standards—that penalized saints and rewarded murderers, that enriched the undeserving and penalized the deserving, and so on. By itself, that yields no particular reason to prefer statism to antistatism, since only a fool would deny that actual states can have the same effects. Indeed, it appears offhand that states are always dangerous to justice in that the extreme concentrations of power they represent can always be turned to unjust ends, so anarchism relieves you of one huge actual barrier to justice. But I do not deny that it might introduce others.

(5) *An anarchism that does not regard human beings exclusively in their economic aspect and does not seek to reduce human action to a single dimension of causation, but rather to recognize a plurality of personalities and motives.*

The exclusive emphasis on class and the identification of persons with economic functions that are characteristic of both communist and capitalist thought, and that were particularly virulent in the nineteenth and early twentieth centuries, is a derangement. Probably on its own account, the view of persons primarily as producers and consumers emerges from specifiable economic conditions. One excellent effect of individualism is that it does not have to perform these sorts of reductions. People's spiritual, moral, or familial commitments are of no less moment in their identities than their professions or their incomes or their class. I seek an individualism of the whole human person, one that is capable of seeing persons in all their aspects and of resolving to let them be. Of course the reduction of human relations to economic relations also tends to run along with an egoistic presumption that people always act in their economic interest as they see it, which is a position that you would not believe except under the influence of an antecedent theory. This is not to say that economic function, status, and even, within limits, class cannot be important in social analysis. But the agency of classes in history must be denied on pain of dictatorship, whether of the proletariat or, more likely, of the plutocrat. We need a nominalism with regard to class as much as with regard to the state and other collective entities.

I might draw attention to one bizarre traditional locution of the left: "the masses." The masses are pictured as revolting, acquiescing, being educated, or whatever. I heard someone today on the radio: "I know individuals can pull themselves up from the bottom, but what about the masses?" as if, after all the individuals pulled themselves up from the bottom, the masses would be left there at the bottom in a kind of quasi-human soup. If you ever find yourself resorting to such a term, pause and try to resolve this soup in your mind into the actual human beings composing it. Try not to think of yourself as the amazing intelligentsia, as the actual individual bringing enlightenment to some undifferentiated, as it were, food-processed humanity. Of course the food processor is primarily economic, and we are all here to uplift or possibly puree "the poor."

I do not believe that people always pursue their own economic interest. I don't even believe they always pursue interest in whatever way this might be construed, or take themselves to be doing so. As I have argued at length in my book *End of Story*, I don't think people arrange their actions through a series of rational calculations. I don't believe the primary bases of our action take place through Aristotelian practical syllogisms or even means/ends calculations broadly construed.

(6)(7) *An anarchism that emphasizes the connections of the individual to other persons as constitutive of individuality, but asserts that an affirmation of individuality is the first moment in re-establishing this connection;*

An anarchism that emphasizes the connection of the individual to the order of nature— to nonhuman creatures and inanimate objects—and its constitution out of such relations.

These claims, I am sure, appear to be in tension with the individualism developed in the previous five. But they are central to the variety of individualism I endorse. I have developed such claims at some length in my previous books; all of my books could be understood as elaborations of the basic insight that a person consists of a web or knot of relations, to give Emerson's formulation.[3] The best way to understand this doctrine is probably through its classic texts, which also happen to be classic texts of a certain kind of nonconformism; it is expressed most intensely in the ancient Taoists, in Native American spiritualities, and in the philosophies of Emerson and Thoreau. As I have already indicated, I regard perception as a process by which a person is penetrated by the external world. If there is no incorporation into the body, there is no perception; light, sound, and taste are aspects of the physical universe that are experienced through their entrance into one's body. This is partly a passive process, but we also direct our bodies into the world by, for example, attention in a way that cultivates experiences or sets a ground for perception. These relations as they accumulate constitute the person. I do not regard the personality or the soul as atomic or changeless in any dimension, as insulated or holding a little kernel of inexplicable essence.

An extremely key aspect or subset of these relations consists of our experiences of persons: we begin life within the body of another, and we communicate continually from before birth. It is obvious that acts of communication flowing in both directions are formative and that they accumulate into a personality. This includes the various "social influences" (about particular ones of which we may raise an ontological skepticism): our class, our school, our religion, our state, our family, and so on. I am perfectly willing to call us "social animals" if we also allow that we are in contact with, and are affected and effected by, other creatures and the inanimate surround. And I am willing to call us social animals only to the extent that this idea is also compatible with the possibility and value of solitude and the possibility and value of dissent with regard to any belief hovering among other people, even among everyone.

These are facts, facts at a level of extraordinary generality, but facts nevertheless. It would be nice if a political philosophy not only acknowledged these facts and was compatible with them, but used them, and used an understanding of the human condition to elaborate that condition in time. They are facts that I insist are compatible with individualism as I understand it. First of all, if the self is constituted in its relations, each self is unique because no two human bodies are in the same set of relations to other things and persons. By the time these relations have articulated an individual over a course of decades, it is massively distinct from any other individual. Think for simplicity's sake of a person as a set of experiences, and experiences as interpenetrations of a human body with what surrounds it. Each experience is unique, though experiences can be similar to one another in the same person or across persons. Then after that person consists of, let's say, a million experiences in a particular order, each of which is itself unique, you have an individual—conceived as a knot of relations—that is massively incomparable. And that incomparable accumulation then performs activities which shape its own further experiences, and so on.

The progress of human life in this sense is a continuous individualization: the longer we live, the less like one another we become. This is a simplistic statement of the sort of view I want to take, which would also take into account the nature of human faculties and would understand experience as a continuous flow of physical penetrations of material that is transformed in the body and re-emerges. But what I need to insist for present purposes is that this understanding of the individual, which is opposed to an egoistic, solipsistic, or atomic conception, is capable of yielding centers of consciousness and moral responsibility. Indeed this is the only sort of process that is capable of such a result.

The various forms of unfreedom attempt to control or homogenize experiences across persons in order to reduce, comprehend, and make use of their individualities. The social analyses that resolve people into demographic segments, including the whole huge machine of census and surveillance, are intended to simplify from or hold in abeyance for the purposes of comprehension the individualities of the people over which they operate. The actual function of power requires the attempt to reduce this individuality, for example to homogenize children or take them en masse in an educational program and to understand them by various numerical measures, which then ground procedures for amelioration. That is, political power sets itself against the process by which a person is simultaneously connected to and individuated within the world. It is important to see that these compromises of individuality are not ways of putting people into relation to one another or the world; on the contrary, to compromise the individuality of persons is to reduce their relations. Individuality has to be conceived as a huge set of particular relations unfolding over time, and to understand people in groups and categories is not to socialize them or bring them to a consciousness of the importance of a collective sense, but to destroy many of the relations between persons that render each person distinct. Marxism does not discover classes and teach solidarity; it manufactures classes by circumscribing relationships and yanks people into pseudo-solidarity by destroying their actual relations.

To say that people are social creatures, a truism of a thousand schools of social critique, is often actually to expunge the bristling particularities of the social relations of each person. To analyze people in groups and as constituted socially or in masses is to attack not only their individuality but precisely their social relations, which must be relations between massively incomparable individualities.

One feature of the schools of thought that assert that "people are social animals" is that they usually ignore the other relations by which human beings are constituted. I suppose the idea is that it is social facts that provide the lens through which all other facts or situations are experienced—language, above all. There is no experiencing a tree before you learn the social conventions for picking out trees, and, once you do, there is no experiencing a tree outside these conventions. I don't really understand what is at stake in the claim that experience derives in its entirety from social conventions, or why people would insist on this or want to believe it. I don't understand how it is possible to believe it. All animals negotiate an environment; language is a means by which we do so, though it might also have other purposes. I guess perhaps the idea is to clear persons of all other relations, reasons, and claims in order to emphasize the entire subordination of persons to cultures. Perhaps not; it hardly matters as long as you still feel the ground beneath your feet. The external world is perceived in the same way other people are perceived: it provides us the structures of experience in the way other people provide us structures of experience; it is in as real interaction with us as other people are. The truth of anarchism doesn't, of course, rest on such claims, but historically the picture of human beings as exclusively constituted by their relations to other human beings is a prelude to totalitarianism and an imaginary detachment from nature that neutralizes the importance, to us, of all the nonhuman things that surround us and that we need and that enter into us and help to create us.

Show me a totalitarian state and I will show you an ecological disaster: the power-madness that is exercised over human beings is exercised over nonhuman beings as well. Show me a people who do not regard themselves as autonomous, who regard themselves as the merest products of culture and subalterns of the state, and I will show you a people careless of or indifferent to the state of the nonhuman world. The anarchism I am proposing would propose a more delicate or slower or more careful attention to the details of our relations to all things.

(8) *An anarchism that is not an amoralism or an immoralism or a libertinism but is compatible with and encourages conscience and self-discipline.*

The individualist tradition with which I associate myself originates in the Protestant Reformation. Even in its most pronouncedly anarchistic moments, this tradition does anything but foreswear ethical judgment; indeed, the position emerges from a certain ethical orientation. This could be summed up in Luther's doctrine of "the priesthood of all believers"—the idea that each person has a primary relation to God, and is responsible for its conduct. Such an idea stands at the bottom of Luther's "justification by faith"—the claim that it is one's identity, not one's social role, which is the moral heart of the matter. Luther himself, of course, stopped far short of the anarchist implications of these doctrines, but they were immediately taken up by the most radical factions of the Reformation and in the subsequent development of Protestantism. The priesthood of all believers leads directly to what came to be called "freedom of conscience," which lies at the heart of modern democratic theory. We have already developed this theme briefly. One outgrowth of this is the moral theory of Kant. Robert Paul Wolff has argued that the political state is incompatible with the moral autonomy of human beings, and hence is incompatible with real freedom and responsibility, using all these terms within a Kantian frame of reference.[4] The moral exhortations of William Lloyd Garrison, for instance, were always aimed at asserting both the freedom and responsibility of his readers; it aimed to show their collusion with slavery in their support of the political state. This is, of course, also the tone of Thoreau's "Civil Disobedience."

One way I might put this is that only when we cease to live under conditions of coercion can we be said to have the chance to achieve moral maturity and to fully take responsibility for ourselves. Only to the extent that we are politically free, to the extent that our actions reflect our choices, can our actions show forth their full moral significance. In criminal procedures one is held responsible for one's actions, but if convicted one is simultaneously relieved of responsibility. The condition of the prisoner is one of circumscribed responsibility because of a supervised scope of freedom, and to the extent that the condition of each of us approaches the condition of a prisoner, to that extent are we morally diminished.

One key impulse that lies at the origin of the state is the desire to dominate and exploit. But the concomitant desire is the impulse to compromise one's freedom in order to reduce the dread that comes with the idea of moral responsibility. This is the collusion in power of the powerless: a desire for freedom from responsibility itself, a retreat to the moral status of a child. This is precisely the direction wherein lies libertinism, or the infinitely large realm of the decadent and the louche, which Protestantism associated with the Catholic Church. One absolves oneself in virtue of one's unfreedom.

On a very wide scale, this can lead to a situation in which terrible evil is done by what is evidently a collective decision: the mobilization of Germany to slaughter Jews, for instance, or the more mundane decision to go to war in a given set of circumstances. Yet no one, or only a few power-mad people, is responsible for what everyone is doing, despite the fact that everyone is actually complicit in doing it. Hitler has the status of mighty, beloved leader, but also the status of sacrificial lamb: his extreme decisions, apparently committing millions of people to action, bring upon himself the responsibility of those people; his responsibility fantastically coincides with the scope of freedom of all the German people. His function is as much to be blamed as to be followed. This is, writ large, the typical relation of human beings to their governments: they complain and acquiesce continually and simultaneously. The complaint is specifically a denial of responsibility.

The radical Reformation tried to put each person in charge of his own relation to God, which is to say, it tried to make each person responsive to his own conscience. The barrier to this was "popery," or the gigantic spiritual and political bureaucracy of the Catholic Church. To make people responsible, the Reformation had to set them free. To reveal persons as moral subjects, it had to deny the justice of their spiritual subjection. In the Lutheran lay preacher Kierkegaard, for example, we see this orientation at its most extreme: our constraints on one another—our conventionality and our laws and our etiquette—hide us from God, and the task we are given as human beings is to become apparent before God by fully understanding our own freedom and responsibility.

This is only one of many strands of anarchist theory, of course, and there are various antipuritan strands in anarchism, many anarchists who think work is wrong or who envision a utopia for their libidos. But it is worth remembering the beautiful effects of puritan anarchists: Christian pacifists such as Garrison, Adin Ballou, Leo Tolstoy, and Dorothy Day; pantheists or something such as Thoreau and Emerson; atheists such as Voltairine de Cleyre. These people did not recognize their duty to obey you, because they were dedicated to mastering themselves; their recommendation of external anarchy is a concomitant to their self-control, and they deny the legitimacy of anyone's control over them in virtue of what they conceive to be the exclusive duty they are under to control themselves.

(9) *An anarchism that does not prescribe any particular set of social arrangements but leaves such arrangements to the voluntary decisions of individuals.*

It will seem trivial to someone who has read this book that its author endorses (9), yet this is the heart of the matter. As we have seen particularly with regard to justicial justifications of state power, to describe an ideal set of social arrangements or distribution is to beg the question against anarchism, because one must envision constituting a power capable of realizing that arrangement. Within political philosophy, anarchism is the position that we should let go and see what happens.

This means that anarchism cannot be the rival of any theory of justice. Anarchism, rather, constitutes the realm that is as a whole the rival of the realm of theories of justice. It corresponds to a noninstrumental consciousness of our relations to one another and to the world. It is a sort of consciousness that does not set an ideal and then try to force the world into that configuration, but allows the world and ourselves to grow wild.

notes

INTRODUCTION

1. Thomas Paine, "Common Sense," *Common Sense and the Crisis* (New York: Doubleday and Company, 1960 [1776]), p.13.

2. Ralph Waldo Emerson, "Politics," from *Essays: Second Series*, *Emerson: Essays and Lectures* (New York: Library of America, 1983), 565–66.

CHAPTER 1.
SOME DEFINITIONS

1. Friedrich A. Hayek, *The Constitution of Liberty* (Chicago: University of Chicago Press, 1978 [1960]), p. 12.

2. Martin van Creveld, *The Rise and Decline of the State* (Cambridge: Cambridge University Press, 1999), p. 1.

3. Bertrand de Jouvenel, *On Power: The Natural History of its Growth* (Indianapolis: Liberty Fund, 1999 [1945]), pp. 99–100.

4. Thomas Hobbes, *Leviathan* (New York: Penguin, 1968 [1651]), pp. 217–18.

CHAPTER 2.
SOCIAL CONTRACT

1. The classic attack is David Hume's "Of the Original Contract," which also provides the classic utilitarian approach to the justfication of state power: "The face of the earth is continually changing, by the increase of small kingdoms into great empires, by the dissolution of great empires into smaller kingdoms, by the planting of colonies, by the migration of tribes. Is there anything discoverable in all these events but force and violence?" ("Of the Original Contract," 1748 [widely republished]).

Lysander Spooner's *No Treason*, no. 2 is an attack specifically on the idea that the American Constitution is a social contract, but it also punctures many of the general pretensions of the theory:

> Thus the whole [American] Revolution turned upon, asserted, and, in theory, established, the right of each and every man, at his discretion, to release himself from the support of the government under which he had lived. And this principle was asserted, not as a right peculiar to themselves, or to that time, or as applicable only to the government then existing; but as a universal right of all men, at all times, and under all circumstances. The agreement [to establish a government] is a simple one, like any other agreement. It is the same as one that should say: We, the people of the town of A——, agree to sustain a church, a school, a hospital, or a theatre, for ourselves and our children. Such an agreement clearly could have no validity, except as between those who actually consented to it. If a portion only of "the people of the town of A——," should assent to this contract, and should then proceed to compel contributions of money or service from those who had not consented, they would be mere robbers; and would deserve to be treated as such. . . . The number who actually consented to the Constitution of the United States, at the first, was very small. Considered as the act of the whole people, the adoption of the Constitution was the merest farce and imposture, binding upon nobody. The women, children, and blacks, of course, were not asked to give their consent. In addition to this, there were, in nearly or quite all the States, property qualifications that excluded probably one half, two thirds, or perhaps even three fourths, of the white male adults from the right of suffrage. And of those who were allowed that right, we know not how many exercised it. Furthermore, those who originally agreed to the Constitution could thereby bind nobody that should come after them. They could contract for nobody but themselves. They had no more natural right or power to make political contracts, binding upon succeeding generations, than they had to make marriage or business contracts binding upon them. (In *The Lysander Spooner Reader*, San Francisco: Fox and Wilkes, 1998 [1867], p. 66.)

William Godwin, *Enquiry Concerning Political Justice*: "If you demand my assent to any proposition, it is necesssary that the proposition should be stated simply and clearly. . . . What then can be more absurd than to present to me the laws of England in fifty volumes folio, and call upon me to give an honest and uninfluenced vote on their contents?" (*Anarchist Writings of William Godwin*, Peter Marshall, ed., London: Freedom Press, 1986 [1793], pp. 92–93)

A. John Simmons, *Moral Principles and Political Obligations* (Princeton: Princeton University Press, 1979), chapters 2–4.

Randy Barnett, *Restoring the Lost Constitution*, chapters 1 and 2:

> There is considerable irony in the assertion of "tacit" consent as the source of the duty to obey the laws. Many who assert this would never accept so atten-

uated a notion of consent to justify, say, the lease of a television. . . . For every-day contract [many legal thinkers] would require "complete information" of everything one is consenting to (or giving up) and a diversity of sufficiently attractive choices before concluding that consent justifies enforcement. Unless these conditions are met, they insist that such consent is "fictitious" or "coerced." Yet we are asked to accept the proposition that merely in virtue of living in the town in which we were born, or by failing to leave the country, we have "consented" to obey nearly any command that is enacted by the reigning legal system. And the consent of a majority is supposed to bind not only themselves, but dissenters and future generations as well. (Princeton: Princeton University Press, 2004, p. 24)

2. John Locke, *The Second Treatise of Government* (Indianapolis: Bobbs-Merrill, 1942 [1690]), p. 4.

3. Harry Frankfurt, "Alternate Possibilities and Moral Responsibility," *Journal of Philosophy* 66 (December 1969), 828–839 (widely anthologized).

4. Aristotle, *The Politics*, Book 1 (1253a1). In *The Complete Works of Aristotle*, ed. Jonathan Barnes (Princeton: Princeton University Press, 1984), pp. 1987–88.

5. Jean-Jacques Rousseau, *The Social Contract*, trans Maurice Cranston (New York: Penguin, 1968 [1762]) pp. 60–61.

6. G. W. F. Hegel, *Philosophy of Right*, trans T. M. Knox (Oxford: Oxford University Press, 1949), p. 183.

7. Charles Taylor, "Hegel: History and Politics," in Michael Sandel, ed., *Liberalism and its Critics* (New York: New York University Press, 1984), p. 181.

CHAPTER 3.
UTILITARIAN JUSTIFICATIONS OF STATE POWER

1. Jeremy Bentham, "A Fragment on Government," 1776. <http://www.ecn.bris.ac.uk/het/bentham/government.htm>, sections 39–42.

2. David Hume, "Of the Original Contract," 1748. Edited by John Roland. <http://www.constitution.org/dh/origcont.htm>.

3. See J. M. Buchanan, *The Limits of Liberty* (Chicago: University of Chicago Press, 1975), chapters 4, 5.

4. Jeremy Bentham, "Panopticon," in Miran Bozovic (ed.), *The Panopticon Writings* (London: Verso, 1995), 29–95.

5. Michel Foucault, *Discipline and Punish*, trans. Robert Hurley (New York: Vintage, 1995 [1975]).

CHAPTER 4.
JUSTICIAL JUSTIFICATIONS OF STATE POWER

1. Plato, *The Republic*, Book 4 (433a). In *The Collected Dialogues of Plato* (Princeton: Princeton University Press, 1961), p. 674ff.

2. John Rawls, *A Theory of Justice* (Cambridge: Harvard University Press, revised edition, 1999), p 96.

3. Herbert Hart, "Are There Any Natural Rights?" *Philosophical Review*, 1955.

4. Robert Nozick, *Anarchy, State, and Utopia* (New York: Basic Books, 1974), chapter 5.

5. Henry David Thoreau, "Civil Disobedience," in, e.g., *Thoreau: Collected Essays and Poems* (New York: Library of America, 2001 [1848]), p. 216.

6. Nozick, 163 ff.

7. Michael Sandel, *Liberalism and the Limits of Justice* (Cambridge: Cambridge University Press, 1982), p. 173.

8. Jürgen Habermas, *Between Facts and Norms* (Boston: MIT Press, 1998), p. 448.

9. Randy Barnett, *Restoring the Lost Constitution* (Princeton: Princeton University Press, 2004), p. 39.

CHAPTER 5.
SILHOUETTE OF AN ANARCHISM

1. Henry David Thoreau, *A Week on the Concord and Merrimack Rivers*, in *Thoreau* (New York: Library of America, 1985), p. 104.

2. Friedrich Nietzsche, *Thus Spoke Zarathustra*, trans. Walter Kaufmann (New York: Penguin, 1978), p. 49.

3. "A man is a bundle of relations, a knot of roots, whose flowers and fruitage is the world." Ralph Waldo Emerson, "History," *Essays: First Series*, in *Emerson: Lectures and Essays* (New York: Library of America, 1978 [1841]), p. 254.

4. Robert Paul Wolff, *In Defense of Anarchism* (Berkeley: University of California Press, 1998 [1970]).

index